God Said

By

Thressa Gillespie

1663 Liberty Drive, Suite 200
Bloomington, Indiana 47403
(800) 839-8640
www.AuthorHouse.com

© 2005 Thressa Gillespie. All Rights Reserved.

No part of this book may be reproduced, stored in a retrieval system, or transmitted by any means without the written permission of the author.

First published by AuthorHouse 09/02/05

ISBN: 1-4184-8464-4 (sc)

Printed in the United States of America
Bloomington, Indiana

This book is printed on acid-free paper.

DEDICATION

(1Corinthians 16:9)
For a great door and effectual is open to me, and there are many adversaries.

Ebony Seagraves

I didn't know the first thing about writing a book or how to begin to put it together. I did know that it had to be a power greater than myself for me to have such a vision.
I was just a strung out addict looking for my next hit, but God placed a dream inside of me.
However, there was one problem I had given up on my dreams.
God gave me a vision before I could understand what a vision was.
He gave me a glimpse of my future while I was still an addict.
Because I didn't have anything to use for comparison except my past, in my eyes, I had nothing to live for.
I knew that inside of me was a good person, but if a person couldn't see past my addiction he or she will miss the good part of me.
When God began to give me poetry, I listened and wrote.
Before I knew it, this book was completed.
I had never in my life heard poems so beautiful, and this poetry was coming through someone like me.

(1Corinthians 1:27)
But God hath chosen the foolish things of the world to confound the wise; and God has chosen the weak things of the world to confound the things, which are mighty.

God placed a special little girl in my life. Her name was Ebony. She was my niece. She respected me and loved me just as I was. She did not judge me. She started helping me to rewrite the poems that I heard in my head and put on paper. She was about 11 years old. I remember our sitting down and rewriting poems to make them legible so that someone else could read them. Mind you, I didn't start out writing a book.
I was just writing what I heard God say to me.

Over a period of years, I realized that there were enough poems for a book.
Writing a book was something that no one in our family had ever done. Ebony found it very exciting. It was new to both of us. However, I was finally beginning to see that God had given me a gift. Writing poetry was a talent God had given to me to minister to so many other people to show God's delivering power. Ebony is now 20 years old, and I love her very much.
Ebony, always keep yourself where God can use you. You were a blessed child, and you grew up to be a beautiful young lady.
May God be your guide? May He alone order your footsteps, and may His peace and wisdom be with you all the days of your life. May the glory of God rest upon you. Ebony, you have been such a blessing in my life, and I will never forget you for that.
You will always be in my prayers. I love you now and forever.
Love Thressa Gillespie

ACKNOWLEDGEMENT

1 John 2:28 and now, little children abide in him; that, when he shall appear, we may have confidence, and not be ashamed before him at his coming.

God is the first Person that I want to acknowledge. These are His poems. He put the words in my head and gave them meaning and now they can touch the lives of people all over the world.
I acknowledge Him because without Him there would be no book. If God had not come into my life when He did, I would not be here today.
I thank God for coming into my life and bringing significance to it.

Pastor Michael Thomas

Ephesians 4:15-
16: "But speaking the truth in love, may grow up into him in all things, Which is the head, even Christ. From whom the whole body fitly joined together and compacted by that which every joint supplieth, according to the effectual working in the measure of every part, maketh increase of the body unto the edifying of itself in love".

At the time I was writing this book, Pastor Michael Thomas, was my pastor an upright and God-fearing man, a man that loves God's people and desires to see growth.
I thank God that he's not a people pleaser, but wants to see the will of God moving in the lives of God's people. God has blessed me by placing godly leaders in my life that so that I may accomplish what He has purposed me to do.
Because of the teaching that I have received at this church, I can apply it and walk in what God has called me to do, which is being able to bring God's vision to past for my life.
Romans 10:17 so then faith cometh by hearing, and hearing by the word of God.
Thank you for keeping yourself where you can hear from God and having the passion to pour into the lives of others.
This ministry has changed my life and the words God speak through you has giving me a new way of living.

Exodus 33:17-19 And the Lord said unto Moses, I will do this thing also that thou has spoken: for thou has found grace in my sight, and I know thee by name. And he said, I beseech thee, shew me thy glory. And he said, I will make all my goodness pass before thee, and I will Proclaim the name of the Lord before thee and will be gracious, to whom I will be gracious and will show mercy on whom I will shew mercy.

Barbara Washington

(Numbers 6:24-26)
The Lord bless thee, and keep thee:
The Lord make his face shine upon thee, and be gracious unto thee:
The Lord lift up his countenance upon thee, and give thee peace.

Barbara has truly been a blessing in my life. Not only is she my attorney but also she has become a very good friend. Barbara came in my life as a member of the Drama Ministry. We both had parts in a play. During the many hours of rehearsal, we got to know each other. Barbara has a very special place in my heart and I will never forget her love and kindness and all the joy she has brought into my life. She began to help me to bring this vision to pass, and because of her willingness to help me, I will be ministering to the world through poetry.
Barbara, may God give you your heart's desire and be a light in your path all the days of your life. May God bless every step you take? Thank you for helping me bring this vision to pass.

Patrick Tuttle & Billy Barrier

(Proverbs 16:3)
Commit thy works unto the Lord, and
Thy thoughts shall be established.

Patrick Tuttle & Billy Barrier are two dedicated young men that have become a blessing in my life, when I began to work on this book. They were very patient with me in the designing of the cover. This book cover was designed from a picture in my head. They completed the Book Cover and it was just as I envisioned. This is an area where they are looking to do more work. These are two wonderful artists, and I was

blessed the day they came Into my life and it will be a blessing to you also. May God open doors and use you in ways that you never dreamed. I pray you get as much work as you desire in this area. Patrick and Billy thank you so much for your commitment and hard Work, to get this book finished, and may God bless the works of your hands.
I thank God everyday for placing not one but two wonderful artists in my life and I will always remember the wonderful spirit I see in the both of you. God bless you both.

Mary Rucker

(Psalm 84:11)
For the Lord God is a sun and shield; the
Lord will give grace and glory: no good
thing will he withhold from them that walk uprightly.

Mary has been a wonderful friend to me. I had never had a person in my life that treated me so well spiritually, financially and personally.
She was there for me through my transitional stage, which was one of the hardest times in my life. She poured into my life all the way and she taught me what a real friend is. I thank God everyday for placing her in my life.
She also understood when I grew in the Lord that I wouldn't be so needy. She watched me leave the nest and that was fine with her she understood that when God came into my life that there would be change and she welcomed it. Today, she still prays for me and pours into my life, but the now the difference is that I too can pray and pour back into her life.
Mary, thank you for investing in my life. You made an investment in me even when people thought that you were wasting your time. You never wavered as my friend.
You are a true friend. As you read this book, I hope that you can now see the fruit of your labor. I pray that God will give you the desires of your heart.

Edited by Joyce Jones

(Matthews 6:33-34) *but seek first his kingdom and his righteousness,* **and all these things** **will be given to you as well. Therefore do not worry about tomorrow, for tomorrow will worry about itself. Each day has enough trouble of its own.**

Joyce thank you for investing your time to help my vision come to pass. I don't think you will ever know what you have done for me and words cannot express it. May God order each and everyone of your footsteps and may every door God has for you in the future open and you will not hesitate about walking into them.

Each of these people played an important role in birthing this book. Lord, my prayer for each one of these people is that you will bless them above and beyond what they could think, pray or imagine. Lord pour them out a blessing that they won't have room enough to receive. In Jesus' Name I pray, Amen.

(Psalm 37:11) But the meek shall inherit the earth; and Shall delight themselves in the abundance of peace.

FROM THE AUTHOR:

(Isaiah 43:19) Behold, I will do a new thing
Now it should spring forth; shall ye not know it?
I will even make a way in the wilderness, and
Rivers in the desert.

God has blessed me to write this poetry.
He could have chosen anyone, but I am glad he chose me.
I just need to make sure you understand, just because God called you to
do something doesn't mean you will always want to do it.
When God began to give me poetry and waking me up at
2 and 3am in the morning I didn't want to wake up or write.
I wanted to sleep, But...I realized very quickly
I wouldn't able to sleep until I did what God wanted me to do.
Over the years I began to accept the gift God had given me and
It has become my passion; I can't imagine my life without poetry.
I am now open and ready to allow God to use
me to minister to people in all walks of life.
I don't have to even know them for God to minister to them.
God gave me purpose when he called me to write.
For the first time in my life I felt I was born for a reason.
God has birthed several books in me
And they will be life changing for the people God has
Called them to minister to.
Matthew 20:16 so the last shall be first, and
The first last: for many are called but, few
Are chosen
God not only called me, but he chose me.

INTRODUCTION

Joel (2:25-26) I will restore the years that the locust has eaten, the
Cankerworm, and, and the caterpiller, and the
Palmerworm, my great army which I seen among you.
And yea shall eat in plenty, and be satisfied, and praise
The name of the Lord your God that has dealt wondrously
With you: and my people shall never be ashamed.

This is not just another book; this book was designed to reach places in your life that no man can reach. In this book God will speak right to you about your past and your future, and this will bring forth potential that you never knew was there.

God will take you into your destiny and you will walk into your new Identity that God has purposed for your life even before your birth. Even I as the writer was ministered to while writing this book. This book is designed to expose painful areas in your life so you can allow the Lord to begin to heal you. It's not because I wrote it, but because God has breathed on it, anointed it, has his hand is on it that He desires to set you free.

I just want to make sure you understand, I can't take any credit for anything you are about to read. True there is a lot of poetry in this book that comes from my experiences, but what you don't understand is that I had all of this stuff inside my head.

Most of my life I was very confused, because I didn't know how to separate it or express it. God put all these words into poetry and called it ministry. Now God uses it to minister to people in all walks of life. There is no such thing as a helpless case, it's just that man doesn't have all the answers.

(Jeremiah 1:5) Before I formed the in the belly I knew thee and before thou camest forth out of the womb I sanctified thee, and I ordained thee a prophet unto the nations.

This book will have you digging inward in area's where things are hidden so deep, that it isn't even visible to you anymore. Situations from your past that you promised yourself to never remember or acknowledge again. I'm talking about the things you pretend never happened. The things you've said you dealt with, but you only covered it up. Because of the walls you have built up you will find yourself questioning where your life went wrong. It will cause you to look back and uncover things that you thought was best left behind. In my experience, once I received Christ, He began to heal me. It was past hurts I needed to deal with and this was very painful. There were people from my past that I didn't want to forgive?

(Ephesians 4: 31) Let all bitterness, and wrath, and anger and clamour, and evil speaking, be put away from you with all malice:

I found everything I was trying to run from I had to face it head on. These were my demons that kept me dependent on drugs. God requires me to forgive anyone who has hurt or harmed me. Not for them, but for me.

(Philippians 3: 13-14) Brethren, I count not myself to have apprehended: but this one thing I do, forgetting those things which are behind, and reaching forward unto those things, which are before, I press toward the mark for the prize of the high calling of God in Christ Jesus.

All this confusion kept me in bondage. For forty years I carried this pain not knowing it was destroying me.

I never connected depression, stress, physical pain or mental distress, with my past hurts, but I always felt my past was never to far behind. I know now that everything that I have been through will be an instrument that God can use to be a blessing in the lives of others. Once God opened my eyes to the truth, I learned, my past will never change, and I don't have to allow it to dictate my future.

God looked past my faults and saw my needs. You can't be confused about this: Being exposed to the truth can mean life or death to you. So hear what I am about to say.

You have to be healed of your past in order to be effective in your future in the Kingdom of God.

So other people may be healed, delivered and set free. How can you tell people God can heal, deliver and set you free if you're still bound? Whether you know it or not the world is watching us to see if they can see God, but "What are they seeing through your lifestyle?" Be honest with yourself, if someone was living your lifestyle and you weren't saved could they draw you into the Kingdom of God? I not only thank God for what he is doing in my life, but what he is doing in the lives of others and for such an important work he has entrusted me to. I am truly grateful. I just wanted to see God's hand move in my life and in the lives of others. I also realized that once I received Christ the healing process began but it wasn't going to make everything easy. Once God began to show me the purpose of my life I became a better person because I then understood how effective it would be in the kingdom of God. If I couldn't stop the old things, how could I see the new things that God wanted to add in my life?

There were many times when I felt very lonely and wanted to give up. I cried many nights. Not only did I have to leave all of my past friends, but I also had to leave my family and distance my children. God wanted me to go forward and not backward. I had tried it my way and it wasn't working for me. So I tried it God's way; but it cost me something. To me it was a high price to pay but my life was worth so much more. Today my life has change in a positive way and I am still drug free 5 years. God has placed some wonderful people in my life. Lord; bless each and every person that was placed in my life to help bring this vision to pass. Lord bless each person according to his or her works. Open up the windows of heavens and pour them out a blessing that they won't have room enough to receive. Give them above and beyond anything they can ask or pray in Jesus name; Amen. Thank all of you so much for what you have added to my life and I will never forget you. May God send? the people in your life that will help to bring your visions to pass. God desires to heal deliver and set you free. Yes you! It's your time! Will you answer Him? Will you hear Him when He calls you?

The ball is in your court. Who will you serve? Life Or Death.

(Exodus 14:14) The Lord shall fight for you, and ye shall hold your peace.

PART 1:
THE FAMILY COLLECTION

(Habakkuk 2:3)
For the vision is for an appointed time, but at the end it shall speak, and not lie, though it tarry,
Wait for it because it should surely come, it will not tarry.

TABLE OF CONTENTS

DEDICATION v
ACKNOWLEDGEMENT vii
FROM THE AUTHOR: xi
INTRODUCTION xiii

WEDDING POEMS 1
    BE MINE 3
    TRUE LOVE 4
    BE BLESSED 5
    A LOVE THAT LASTS 6
    PERFECTED LOVE 7
    WE ARE ONE 8
    LET THERE BE 9
    SOLD OUT 10
    CALLED 11

BABY POEM 13
    A HEAVENLY CONVERSATION 15

ANNIVERSARY POEMS 17
    A LOVE STORY 19
    YOU SAID 20

BIRTHDAY POEMS 21
    THAT'S WHAT LOVE IS ABOUT 23
    RIGHT FROM THE HEART 24
    I FOUND LOVE IN YOU 25

MOTHER'S DAY POEMS 27
    A RARE PEARL 29
    IN THE MASTERS HAND 30

A MOTHER'S LOVE	31
FIRST LOVE	32
FATHER'S DAY POEM	**33**
IN HIS IMAGE	35
GRADUATION POEM	**37**
CONGRATULATIONS ARE IN ORDER	39
THE MINISTRY COLLECTION	**41**
WOE IT'S ME	43
TODAY	44
I DIDN'T KNOW	45
MY PRECIOUS HEAVENLY TREASURE	46
HE'S REAL	47
ANSWERED PRAYERS	49
GOD'S LOVE	50
CHILDREN OF A KING	52
COME ON IN	53
GOD'S GRACE	54
HEAR MY VOICE	55
UNSPEAKABLE JOY	56
CHOSEN ONE	57
FAITHFUL SERVANT	58
YOU'RE THE APPLE OF MY EYE	59
MAKING THE DIFFERENCE	60
LOVE AT LAST	61
MY CHILD	62
FAITHFUL ONE	63
GIVE IT TO ME	64
PERFECTION DESIRED	65
WORD UP	66

APPRECIATION POEMS 67
- MY GIFT 69
- EARTHLY TREASURES 70
- A PETITION TO HEAVEN 71
- IT TAKES TWO 72

DELIVERANCE POEMS 73
- PERSONAL PRAYER 75
- WHO AM I 76
- THEY CALL ME ADDICTION 77
- COCAINE'S TRUTH OR CONSEQUENCES 79
- LORD HEAR MY CRY 81
- THE DOPE MAN 82
- WHAT DO I HAVE TO LOSE 84
- WANTED 85

BEREAVEMENT POEM 87
- PURPOSE FULFILLED 89

HEALING POEMS 91
- FAITH IS BLIND, BUT THE SPIRIT CAN SEE 93
- HALF A WOMAN 94
- SEARCHING 95
- I DARE NOT DREAM 96
- AT LAST 98
- LETTING GO 99
- FOLLOW ME 100
- ANOTHER CHANCE 101
- QUALITY GOLD 103
- I FORGIVE 104
- BROKEN 105
- COME IN 106
- REAL LOVE 107

    WHERE IS THE LOVE 108
    HOLD ON 109
    HIDDEN LOVE 110
    BE HEALED 111
    BLINDED 113
    BROKEN HEARTED 114
    YOU'RE SPECIAL 115
    SALVATION 116
    BRO-KEN LO-VE 118
    ALONE 119

VALENTINE POEMS 121
    MY LOVE 123
    CAN'T NOBODY LOVE YOU LIKE ME 124
    BE MY VALENTINE 125

PASTOR POEMS 127
    SENT BY GOD 129
    PURE GOLD 130

RESTORATION POEMS 131
    WAIT I SAY ON THE LORD 133
    I'LL SEND HIM 134
    GOD CAN'T LIE 136
    TRUST ME 137
    BEHOLD MY SON, BE WHOLE 139

Thressa Gillespie

PART 1

WEDDING POEMS

God Said

Thressa Gillespie

BE MINE

My Daughter, you've looked a long time for this special
love you wanted to find; but first my daughter, you had to
be mine before this special love you would find.
My daughter, I only wanted to give you the best
I wouldn't have you settle for less.
All the love you have to give, it is special and very real.
My daughter, this is my son.
He will love you like no other one.
His love is very real,
And when he loves you my daughter, all
your wounds will begin to heal.
Oh, what a joy this day will be.
Watch my children, Wait and See!

TRUE LOVE

You know when I think of you, I feel a love I never knew.
The love that you added to my life, I'd be honored
if you would be my wife.
When I'm with you there's this joy. It's a joy like never before.
You are so special to me. I just want to make sure you see.
The love I have is like none from the past. This love I have is going to last.
I will not cheat or turn away. This love I have for you is here to stay.
I want you to have my best, and my love won't allow me to give you less.
God only gives this special love. It's unconditional love from above.
You can't get it anywhere else I love you as I would love myself.
So in order for this new life to last, your old life
needs to remain in the past.
True love comes from me my child; always remember
your wedding vows.
A wedding is for a love that's true and that's what
I see in the two of you.
Now this my daughter is my son, and when you are
wed you'll become one.
My son, you'll be the man of the house. Make sure my son
you love your spouse.
You are to be responsible my son, because when you say
"I DO" you will become one.

Thressa Gillespie

BE BLESSED

Blessed my children is what this marriage will be
Because this wedding was planned by me.
He who finds a wife finds a good thing.
This beautiful woman my son is your queen.
For all the days that you should live
That unconditional love is what you should give.
You know my daughter, this is my son.
In case you feel unsure, he is the one.
The love he has for you is hard to find anywhere else.
He loves you as much as he loves himself.
My angels came so you both could see
these unseen gifts come from me.
Love each other the way I Love You.
You will seal that love when you say, "I do"
blessed is what this marriage will be
Because this wedding my children was planned by me.

A LOVE THAT LASTS

Today is the day that we become one.
I joined together my daughter and
my son.
What I have joined together let no man put asunder.
The things ahead... what a wonder!
The love you have I can see
because where there is love, there is Me.
The angels in heaven are rejoicing this day.
They are dancing in a heavenly way.
Be happy, have joy, just be free
because you my children can rest in me.
So let your old life be a part of your past
and follow me and your new life will last.
Today my children, my light will shine
Because this day is your time.

Thressa Gillespie

PERFECTED LOVE

I never met a woman until the day I met you.
I never had the desire to ever say, "I do".
The first day that I saw you, I knew you were the one.
It was hard for me to believe that my love had finally come.
God knew what I wanted, but I never had a clue.
He had planned in heaven that He would send me you.
I'm so glad that God understands our detailed life
and I would be honored if you would be my wife.
Every time I think of the day we'll say "I do",
I sometimes wonder if it's a dream
Because I'll be a part of you.
I just want to say you can never be replaced.
Every time I close my eyes I can only see your face.
The empty place in your life, you couldn't seem to fill.
I had the same emptiness, but now I can say I'm healed.
I love you from this day forward as long as we both shall live,
And all the love I have held inside, to only you I'll give.

God Said

WE ARE ONE

Some people feel that true love is in a book.
The reason that they do is because
they are not patient enough to look.
Love is something that is nurtured and true.
That's what I see in the two of you.
You two are special in my sight
because of this you will shine in my light.
This my children is your time
and on this day you're going to shine.
This wedding is like none from before
because you my children want to invest more.
To My son, love your wife
because this son should not happen twice.
My daughter, love my son
because he loves you and chose you to be the one.
Cherish each other as you do me
because when I look at you, one is what I see.
Coming together will make this love complete
because this love my children I know will keep.

Thressa Gillespie

LET THERE BE
Marriage + Jesus = Love

Ingredients:
One man, one woman, enter marriage.
Add salvation, healing, grace, and mercy.
Add prayer, the word, the, anointing and Jesus.
Bake in the spirit and taste and see that the Lord is good.
Ummmmm, it is done… true love

You and I have now become one.
To complete this wedding, we need Jesus the son,
To bring this marriage under the blood
and give birth to a new way to love.
There is something special about the two of you,
and God only wants the best for you.
God wants to give you so much joy.
With that come blessings and more.
Purpose is something inside of us all.
The gifts that God gives are anything but small.
I am the Lord God and I called this marriage to be.
Love my children is a gift from me.
My son, you are the king of your castle.
My daughter, you couldn't have chosen anyone better.
If you went around the world from the beginning to the end,
This daughter is where you will end.
In you my daughter I see a queen.
And true love is not only found in dreams.
This love that I speak of is rarely seen.
This special love was created for queens.
When I look at you, one is what I see.
This my children are who I've called you to be.
This love is found in Jesus you see.
So this is your invitation to be set free.
Make sure my children, you understand.
True love just can't be found in a mere man.
True love my children can be found in me.
It can be expensive, but I'll give it to you free
if you pick up your cross, and follow me.

SOLD OUT

My son, I just want you to know, you sold out
and gave me your soul.
Because of your faithfulness and your love for me,
I've opened your eyes and blessed thee.
I'll pour you out a blessing that you won't have room
enough to receive, and put in your hands the kingdom keys.
This woman that will become a part of your life, whom you
have chosen to be your wife, she will bring you so much joy.
You will love like never before. I am the one that said,
"Let There Be" You heard my voice, and you knew it was me.
Weddings my son was created by me, and this is how
I said it should be.
My son, be the man of your house, and remember
My son to love your spouse.
Make sure that you keep your marriage alive
because you are the one that makes sure it survives.
Tell her the things that she needs to hear; make sure that
she hears you; make sure that it's clear.
Even the things that don't seem like much, say it anyway,
her heart will be touched.
What a joy your new life will be with your new wife, true
love, and most of all me.
My daughter, yes, I have heard your prayers even when
you thought no one was there.
I even know your heart's desires; I've known them
since you were a child.
Love my son with all your heart, and the two of you
will never be apart.
They say a diamond is a woman's best friend.
Well, you will have one until the end.
My daughter and my son, I just want you to know
love is what you were created for.
So love each other as you do me, and let your love shine
for the world to see.

Thressa Gillespie

CALLED

Called my children, you were called by me.
This wedding that you are planning is meant to be.
I planned your future before you even became a seed.
When I called you forth I supplied all your needs.
I smiled upon the two of you
because of the wonderful works that you will do.
The angels are rejoicing in heaven today
because they know that your wedding is on the way.
You my children have both been primed.
This will be such a glorious time.
This wedding will be anointed and you will be blessed
because you my children deserve the best.
There will be no doubt that I called this wedding forth.
It came to past because you both were on course.
Oh my children, what a day this will be
when your future that I speak of, even you will see.
Because you, my son, made Me Lord of your life
you heard my voice and you found a wife.
Because you my daughter stayed on course,
you can say, "I DO" with no remorse.
Thank you my children for loving me first
because loving me is how your wedding was birthed.
And if you, my children, want your wedding to last
keep me first as you have done in the past.

God Said

Thressa Gillespie

BABY POEM

God Said

Thressa Gillespie

A HEAVENLY CONVERSATION

From A Babies Point of view

Before I became a seed, even entering into your womb
I knew that I would be called and I knew it would be soon.
This will be a very special day.
There is something in my heart that I very much need to say.
I love you Mom and Dad in a very special way.
When they said to me in heaven for me to come and see
these two loving parents they were giving to me
I knew when I saw you this was where I wanted to be.
I went right to the Lord and asked, "Oh Lord, please let me".
There are two special people just waiting there for me.
The angels said in heaven, "Even we can see
what a glorious day this is going to be".
When you were sitting and waiting for me to come to pass
I said, "It is time Oh Lord to meet my family at last".
There was a party going on in heaven
because you were about to see
a miracle about to come to past and that miracle would be me.
I am a special seed that the Lord picked right from His hand.
He planted me, He watered me, and He formed me day and night
until the day came that I would come to light.
I remember looking out of heaven's door
seeing the very same love that I had seen before.
I knew that I was special and I would be very loved.
I hugged Jesus one more time and came to a new kind of love.
Congratulations, Mom and Dad, for a gift you now can see.
An angel was sent right from heaven to earth. That angel Mom is me.

God Said

Thressa Gillespie

ANNIVERSARY POEMS

God Said

Thressa Gillespie

A LOVE STORY

This gift that I have for you comes right from my heart.
There is so much I could say, if I only knew where to start.
All the money in the world could not replace your love.
It's a special gift Mom and Dad that you put in all your hugs.
Everything that you've done was in such a special way.
I just want to say that I love you today.
There really are no words to express the way I feel
about all the things you've done in my life, in all
Your wonderful years.
When I look back over the years and the way that
I was raised,
I thank God so very much. It's instilled in me today.
If people only knew how true love is supposed to be.
How I wish they could meet you so that they may see.
I know God had to have brought you and dad together.
This love that I have seen could only come from Heaven.
I'm not sure if I've told you just how much I care.
All I remember was no matter what you were always there.
Mom, I was blessed to be a part of your life, and Dad
was blessed when you became his wife.
To my life was added so much love and joy, and never in a
million years did I think that there could be more? Lord, if
I could ask for anything in life, it would be to have
one hundred and forty years added to their lives.
You know Mom and Dad, I just want to say
Happy Anniversary to both of you today.

YOU SAID

When God created you it was then that I knew
the day that we met we couldn't be two.
The love that was there was easy to see
that God had created you just for me.
So many things I could have done
but in my heart I knew you were the one.
What gift could I give, or what words can I say
to express this love inside of me today?
It's a joy that I have deep down inside.
I know even now God was my guide.
This love that I have grows more and more each day,
and my heart's overjoyed, I must say.
This love that I have for you is such a joy.
Your children would bring me so much more,
another part of you to add to my life
That would make my days pleasantly nice.
Lord, You said that I could have my heart's desire.
You've given me my husband, but I now want a child.
Lord, You said, "Ask and it shall be given".
I'm asking you now I would love to have children.
Lord, today I have released my request.
I know you only want me to have your best.
Lord, You said your word couldn't come back void.
So, I'm asking you now to hear my voice.
I offer my request to you today.
Be my guide and show me the way.
Lord, I'm going to thank you again
for this miracle child you're going to send.

BIRTHDAY POEMS

God Said

Thressa Gillespie

THAT'S WHAT LOVE IS ABOUT

Poems are how I express the way that I really feel.
I thank God for this wonderful gift that He so freely gives.
I would think that my words would soon run out,
But that's what love is all about.
It would have been a shame if I would have never seen
what a wonderful gift you are and your prayers
for me to be clean.
It's something how you protected me, and how
very much you really cared.
Anyone would want a sister like you, but they are very rare.
My heart is just so full no matter what I say.
I can't think of enough words to express my feelings today.
How can God bless one person so very much?
I love you, and you're special to me I love you so very much.
This is a gift that I had sealed deep down within.
I was in so much pain and I was still living my life in sin.
But now God is healing me and beginning to set me free
He took all my guilt and pain so now I may finally see.
I just want to tell you, He loves you just the same.
If no one has ever told you, this is why He came.
I could never compete with you and the gifts that you give,
But poetry is hidden treasure and inside of me it lives.
When I wrote this poem, I just had to cry
because I felt it wasn't special, because it
wasn't something I could buy?
I know I have given you poems over and over again
But there were things that were locked up, and
I felt them deep within.
There is not just one day that my heart desires to give.
If poems are what God gives for you, I'll write them as
long as you live.
Before you know it you'll look around, and my
love will fill your house.
And I will say it again, that's what love is all about.
I just want to see… how I can get this out?
This is a gift from the one who loves you
Because that's what love is all about.

God Said

RIGHT FROM THE HEART

There's a rumor going around and it's about you.
It was something that I wondered about,
but I never really knew.
There were so many things that I wanted to say,
Or just announce to the world. Today's your birthday!
What warm thoughts I had once it reached my heart.
I knew that this was a special day, and I couldn't just give a card.
I just want this birthday to be different from all of the rest
because this year, I'm a part of it, and I wouldn't want to give you less.
I just want to tell you that to me you're more than just a friend.
I love you from my heart and I'll love you until the end.

Thressa Gillespie

I FOUND LOVE IN YOU

Blessings are not always money you see,
but in my life, it was when God gave you to me.
As my mother, my friend, and an angel on earth,
you're the kind of mother that puts her children first.
Love is a word that can't carry a price, but love is what
you've added to our life.
Because of the seeds that you've planted with care,
that love Mom you nourished is still right there.
Some people are not able to experience this joy,
But God gives this love and He has more.
Every year I look for something special for you
this year it's love and it's a gift that's true.
When God sent you from up above
that must have been the day He created love.
You know things were never to be the same,
because on that day my whole life would change.
True love is a gift that's hard to find,
but mom we don't have to look, you're love all the time.

God Said

Thressa Gillespie

MOTHER'S DAY POEMS

God Said

Thressa Gillespie

A RARE PEARL

God has given a gift to the world,
A mother to the children; He's given a rare pearl.
A mother is someone that always cares.
No matter what's going on she is always there.
She will stick right by you from the beginning to the end.
She will be there with you through thick and thin.
A mother will pray for you while you're in your sin.
God put this kind of love within.
This special love comes from up above.
Only God gives this special love.
What do you think a mother is for?
She's for that and so much more.
Special is a word that I could use.
Wonderful, loving I could also choose.
But, a rare and special pearl is the word I'll use.
God gave me a gift; He gave me you.
But if I had to choose, I would choose you too.
This gift He gave didn't come from man.
God holds these pearls in the palms of His hand.
If you have a mother in here today,
Why don't you just turn to her and say,
"Mom, I love you in a very special way".
Those of you that have lost this joy,
God said that's what He is here for.
So for all of you that feel you're alone,
I just want to tell you that you are wrong.
You have more love than ever before
Because God is love and so much more.

God Said

IN THE MASTERS HAND

Mom and Dad, I wouldn't trust just anyone with your life.
But, I have placed the two of you in the Master's Hands for life.
That's because I love you and I know God loves you too.
He's the only man that I know that has a love that's true.
I know Jesus to be real and an important part of my life.
And because He is so good to me, I thought
sharing Him would be nice.
Mom, let me tell you all about the Master's Hand.
And maybe then you can understand, why
I placed you in his hand.
First of all, He's different from any man on earth.
He loves you unconditionally Mom and Dad… and
yes, He loved you first.
Then, He will forget everything you have ever done.
Because He died for our sins Mom, He died for everyone.
Then He opens doors that you thought would always be closed.
Because He's God, and He loves you, these doors no man can close.
Dad, I'm just beginning you might have to sit down.
God will never leave you if you need Him, He is always around.
Mom, oh Mom, the love, it covers a multitude of sins,
And His love is unconditional He'll love you until the end.
All of your hurts and pains, he will nurse them until they heal.
He's the greatest man I know, mom and dad that has ever lived.
He's a patient God; His love is really true.
His love is not selfish and our experience makes each day new.
Look at the scripture about the fish and the bread
and how he multiplied it all and the people that He fed.
Mom, this Man is wonderful and He's also my best friend.
Dad, He is different, I'm telling you, and I'm placing you in His hands.
In the Master's Hand, there's no better place to be.
Oh Mom, I forgot to tell you that He died so that we might be free.
Once you experience His love, you will desire it again and again.
His love is true and wonderful Mom it never ends.
So Mom and Dad, I'm going to leave you… right where
I've been saying.
I'll tell you one more time; Mom and Dad, "I've placed you
in the Master's Hand".

Thressa Gillespie

A MOTHER'S LOVE

Mom, I love you everyday, and not just once a year.
I keep you close in my heart, so you are always near.
Just in case you're wondering somewhere in the back of your mind,
I love you Mom and I always will I'm glad to say that you're mine.
Mom, you didn't stop loving me the times that I did wrong.
I remember your giving me love and advice, the times I felt alone.
When you put your arms around me, you did it with so much care.
What I remember most of all is that you were always there.
Blessed is what my mother is I want the world to see.
God created her on earth so He could give her me.
This love that mom has given me, it is very real.
And I know that she will give it all the days that she lives.
Sometimes we forget how special her love is.
Because mom had given it so freely and it's what she wanted to give.
This is the only love that has come close to God's.
And I found that when I get this love, that's when the healing starts.
Mom, I just want to say, "I love you very much".
When you put your arms around me, I feel your loving touch.
Mom, I just want to thank you for your love once again.
I didn't just have a mother, but I also have a friend.

FIRST LOVE

This love that you gave can come from no one but you.
It's a special love and the first one that I ever knew.
Mom, I just want to thank you for the love you've poured in my life.
And because of the way that you've nurtured me,
I have now Mom become a wife.
The love that you poured into me, I can now pour into my spouse,
and I can bring that same special love into my very own house.
Mom, I just want you to understand how much that you mean to me.
All of the love that you poured in, I want the world to see.
Even when I don't see you and you are not around,
I carry your love deep inside of me. That's where it can be found.
Mom, my husband and I share a special love.
There's an added ingredient, which is Jesus, a Love from above.
Mom, your love + Jesus will give us a stronger love.
Mom, I know it's a blessing that comes from up above.
God has sent me an angel from heaven down to earth.
Mom, I'll do the same thing that you did.
Mom, I'll give him true love first.
I just want to say, "I love you again and again".
And I will never stop loving you because that's what you poured in!

Thressa Gillespie

FATHER'S DAY POEM

God Said

Thressa Gillespie

IN HIS IMAGE

I made you in the image of me.
My son, I came to make sure you see
who I your creator called you to be.
A man is more than just a label.
And you my son must be stable.
A father is more than just a seed.
You're the one my son that feeds.
Feed my word to your children and spouse.
You first my son must clean your house.
Being the man of the house is not to control,
But minister to your family and direct their souls.
You my son should carry the cross,
And make sure that their souls will not be lost.
If you my son put me first,
my image my son will then be birthed.
I am the only Way that they can enter in,
but you must want to come out of sin.
The things that I speak of come from above,
and I my son am the Master of Love.
A Christian is different than those of the world
because they know that God answers prayers.
They know that faith open doors
and with that come blessings and more.
They know that the spirit world is very real
And the devil's job is to destroy, steal and kill.
So now that you know what a father should be,
Put on your Armour and follow me.
It's My Image that the world should see
because I came back to set my people free.

God Said

Thressa Gillespie

GRADUATION POEM

God Said

Thressa Gillespie

CONGRATULATIONS ARE IN ORDER

What a glorious day this will be
because you my child have pleased me.
So many stumbling blocks came in your way,
but you my son are still mine this day.
My angels are around me rejoicing today
because Satan had tried to lead you astray.
My son, when I placed my spirit inside of you
My heart was filled with admiration for you.
you may not fully understand
But I hold you in the palms of my hand.
The enemy will deceive you by your "so-called friends",
But a true friend my son will be there until the end.
My son, you don't need approval from man.
I told you, "I hold you in the palms of my hand".
I have so many wonderful plans for your life,
and the things that the world will offer
I've already paid the price.
I have my angels encamped around you each day
because I love you my son, let me lead the way.
Let me be a light in your path.
The world can't give you the things I have.
My son, allow me to be clear to you
and I will be a part of all that you do.
Quality decisions separate the "men from the boys".
And a real man would know that I am Lord.
In life's everyday ups and downs
whenever you look for Me, I can always be found.
My son, I am pleased and I hope that you see
that this is a glorious day for both you and me.

God Said

Thressa Gillespie

PART 2

THE MINISTRY COLLECTION

God Said

Thressa Gillespie

WOE IT'S ME

Woe it's me; it's me again. I just want to thank you again.
For all the prayers you prayed in my life,
your prayers can't be labeled with a price.
All the things that you have spoken to me...you were
a willing vessel that God used to help set me free.
You saw things inside of me and you opened my eyes so that I could see.
Even though I was in a battle with cocaine
it had to leave in Jesus' name.
Even through it all, God was setting me free.
I was shocked to see who God was calling me to be.
Purpose was why I was called from the womb.
Now I know drugs do not have any room.
I know people are watching to see
if I will fall or remain drug free.
I have the greater one inside of me
and if it's my desire God will keep me.
When they look at me, Christ is who they will see
because I'm God's vessel and I've been set free.
Thank you for yielding to hear God's voice.
I'm so glad that was your choice.
What you did was to open my prison doors.
And when I came out, I knew I needed more.
I just want to say I'm drug free
Because you took the time to water me.
I was at the point of giving up
and you came alone and filled my cup.
It wasn't my will to be that way,
But I can say, "I'm free today".

TODAY

There is something special about today.
Jesus rose out of the grave where he laid.
He hung on the cross for our sins.
When they buried him, they thought that was the end.
He came to earth in flesh you see.
God had him to do that for you and me.
When they covered him thinking his life would end,
it wasn't his time, he rose again.
He did this so that the world could see
He would die so that we might be free.
We must pray for the ones that are still in sin
be a shinning light and bring them in.
Jesus died for all of our sins.
To dress up and eat will not get you in.
He just came so that you might see.
The reason he rose was that we might be free.
These words are being spoken about today.
If you believe in him, he will show you the way.
He rose so that we could see.
Because of his blood, we have the victory.
Now that you know what Easter is about,
we can be a shinning light for others to come out.

Thressa Gillespie

I DIDN'T KNOW

All of the time I wasted by not being your friend,
I was finally able to see the beauty you had within.
You are special and make it easy to see.
I'm glad to say you are a friend to me.
God must have made you from the essence of love
because this can only be a godly love.
If you never hear these words again,
in you, I've found a very special friend.
You really couldn't know how you've blessed my life.
And being around you, makes my days especially nice.

MY PRECIOUS HEAVENLY TREASURE

I knew that you were special, but
there was something I didn't understand.
That you were a heavenly treasure, right from the master's hand.
I knew that nothing could compare to the quality of your life.
There's not a pearl or diamond in the world that
could compare with you in price.
When God began to form you, He knew you were a special child
so He began to mold you, and He then began to smile.
Once He had completed you and saw what He had done,
He said this is a marvelous gift for my one and only son.
When it came close for your time to come to earth,
He said, "I love you very much, and my love I give you first".
So no matter what you go through, don't ever give up hope
because God is your Creator, and He will help you cope.
I just want to tell you that I love you very much.
I wish you all the blessings in the world.
I release God's Loving Touch.

Thressa Gillespie

HE'S REAL

Do you think that I don't see
All of the things you've done for me?
You are very strong in my word.
Your prayers, my child I have heard.
You have been so faithful and true.
I am going to stick close to you.
I told you that you would bring your family in.
This is the start, but it's not the end.
It won't be easy to bring in some,
but I knew when I picked you that you were the one.
You are a fighter and you fight so well.
I don't worry that you will fail.
I know that if you fight you're going to win.
You don't give up, and you'll fight to the end.
Fight for my people and don't give up.
That type of fight will fill your cup.
I'm getting ready to open Heaven's Doors, and
I'll give you so much that you won't need more.
Because of the giving heart that you have,
you will make others smile.
Don't let these treasures turn you around.
I, my child, want to keep you sound.
All of the blessings that I have planned
for you in the past
they will still come, but not too fast.
I want to make sure you know what to do.
I don't want it to overwhelm you.
I have to get your family in line; everything
will come but in my time.
Don't you dare lose your faith!
I want you to know I'm still on the case.
Your family has been cursed from long ago.
You will see a change like never before.
You have been so obedient to me.
I'm going to set all of them free,
If they pick up their cross and follow me.

God Said

I will allow you to bless them all
Because you, my child, know you were called.
I've invested so much in you.
I'll continue to show you what to do.
Now, I want you to deal with your flesh
because all of these blessings will be a test.
Long as I know you are in control
I will continue to give you one hundred fold.
Thank you my child I love you so much.
I'm just giving you my loving touch.
The answers to your prayers are Yes, Yes, Yes,
because you my child are passing the test!

Thressa Gillespie

ANSWERED PRAYERS

Your music my daughter is beautiful to me.
The lyrics from your songs will set people free.
The angels are dancing all around my throne
because you are playing those heavenly songs.
I love you my child. I love you so much.
To you my daughter, I give my heavenly touch.
I don't care what the enemy plans for you,
It won't come to pass - A GIFT FROM ME TO YOU.
I'm going to take you to another level.
This my child has been planned in heaven.
You and your husband will be blessed, blessed, blessed
because you my children are passing the test.
You've worked so hard to bring others' visions to pass,
Your vision too will be part of the past.
You know my daughter; I've heard your prayers.
I answered yours because you answered theirs.
Blessed my child is what you will be
Because when I look at you, I see me.

GOD'S LOVE

Why He loves me, I don't know.
All I know is that I need more.
All this hurt I have got to let go.
I have felt such pain before.
But now I feel real peace inside.
Now I can sit still, sleep and be quiet.
The Lord was with me through all of the bad.
He knew what I was thinking, what was in my head!
I found a friend, a friend so true.
This kind of friend, I never knew.
He's now inside of me. He's inside of you too.
If you want to know this God I know,
Drop to your knees, give it a go.
Give him your heart and all of your love!
He'll give it to the Father above.
So, if you love God and want to be free,
Just say Lord, take it all from me.
Once you say it from the bottom of your heart,
You will receive your "deliverance card".
He will take the pain from your heart
So that you can become healthy, wealthy and smart.
All of those things that kept you depressed,
The Lord will begin to get rid of that mess!
So, when you get ready to give it to God,
Everyone will know that you really are smart!
Watch those people that you hang around
Because some just want to keep you down.
Now that you've heard what I had to say,
This is your first step. You're on your way!
Just open your heart and let Him come in
Because you can't get a better friend.
You see, it's not God that makes a mess of your flesh.
He forgives all of your bad and makes you His best!
So, all of you Christians that are trying to do right,
The first step to that is you must be nice.
No one has the right to give others pain.

When you do, you don't get any gain. God says love my people as I love you.
Then see what we can really do.
You need me and I need you.
Together we can do what we see our Father do.
If you really love me the way you say,
Then let God work through us the right way.
So how do I make it from day to day?
I know that God's love is fulfilling me in every way.

CHILDREN OF A KING

My daughter, you are special, in case you didn't know.
I know you have heard these words before.
Special is what I see when I look at you.
The things that you speak in others lives
to help them through.
I just want to tell you that you make a wonderful friend.
And seeing you in my presence gives me joy within.
When they say that your lifestyle reflects your God.
It's easy to see yours, because of your heart.
I see Christ all over you that's
because He's, in me too.
You make it easy for anyone to see.
But that's who God has called you to be.
Blessed is anyone that you will meet
Because knowing you is such a treat.
I know you're special. I'm just going to
tell you again.
You are special from the outside in.

Thressa Gillespie

COME ON IN

I don't want you to give up.
I want you to know I love you so much.
The devil doesn't want to let you go.
He wants you to stand at the door.
But that's not enough my friend.
I want you to come all the way in.
I want to set you totally free.
I want you my child to work for me.
I'm going to tell you this today.
I Am The Truth, The Light, And The Way.
Anything my child that you ask for,
I'm the one that can open the door.
Aren't you tired of that life you had?
Don't you want to let it stay dead?
You deserve so much more.
I just want to give you joy.
All of the dreams that you've had can come true.
Surrender to me and become brand new.
You will begin to love yourself too.
There are so many blessings that I have for you.
Come on, my son, make this the day.
Come on and let me show you the way.

GOD'S GRACE

Grace is something that can only come from God,
And it's a gift from Him dealing with your heart.
Grace can never come from a man,
because he doesn't have the power.
It's only in God's Hand.
Grace is something that God gives
to people coming out of sin.
He wants you to receive Christ to live within.
Grace is for a person that no longer wants their past,
But instead they choose Christ for a life that lasts.
So if you want to finally be free,
Call on God's grace and He will forgive thee
Not just for that time then.
But if you follow him, it's until the end.

Thressa Gillespie

HEAR MY VOICE

My daughter, I'm calling you by name.
You my daughter are why I came.
To give my life to this dying world.
Your beauty is more precious than pearls.
The beauty you have is for the world to see.
But this marvelous beauty will be found in me.
Your heart is filled with so much joy.
You, my daughter, have heard my voice before.
I won't force you. It's your choice.
I want your love with no remorse.
There are gifts that I have stored up for you.
I even have a love that's true.
All of the things that you've been looking for
I can be that and so much more.
I created you in the image of me.
But your true identity only I now can see.
Come on my child. I am the key.
Blessed is who I called you to be.
My daughter today you have a choice.
Just sit still and listen to hear my voice.

UNSPEAKABLE JOY

I met this old lady as sweet as can be.
The things she said really touched me.
She spoke of people that came in her path.
Criminals to me is what she had said,
But to her they were living souls.
Those two words she spoke so bold.
She was a Marshall. She is now 96 years old.
She saw people as living souls.
She spoke about her life as a young girl.
She felt she was needed in this world.
Now she feels a lot has changed.
She enjoys going down memory lane.
Now she feels that she's a bother.
But that can't be true. She's a child of the father.
She talks about death as if it were her friend.
She says it's time for her life to end.
She says she is tired and wanted to rest.
But she says it's God's will, and He knows what's best.
She'll just stay until He calls her to rest
Because He knows that she has given her best.

Thressa Gillespie

CHOSEN ONE

You are more valued than gold.
When God made you, He broke the mold.
You will spread God's word through songs and plays.
People will know you in so many ways.
The angels are in Heaven rejoicing and gay.
The Lord was in Heaven waiting for this day.
You are a blessing in more ways than one.
Just look around and see what you have done.
You will take demons and send them to HELL.
The devil won't be able to cause you to fail.
The Lord will say victory has finally come.
There's no stopping you. Now you've finally won.
My purpose for this earth is what you have done.
This is only the beginning. People of
the world, souls will be won.
You will be blessed from this day on
Because in you, my child, a warrior was born.
Since you have worked so hard for me,
I just want to bless thee.
Anything that may bother you or keep you down,
Give it to me. I'll cast it down.
Don't let my words go to waste.
With you my child, everything will fall in place.
I want to bless you and give you the best
Because you my child are passing the TEST.

FAITHFUL SERVANT

Isaiah 40:31 "But they that wait upon the Lord shall renew their strength; they shall mount up with wings as eagles; they shall Run, and not be weary; and they shall walk, and not faint".

Do you think that I don't see all
of the things that you do for me?
People may say that you are wasting your time,
But loving me is not a crime.
All of the people that have put you down,
I will show them what you have found.
There is nothing that you have to do
Because if I say it, then it's true.
I, my child, have seen your heart,
And you my child have done your part.
It's time for you to take your place
Because I, my child, am on your case.
I know all of your heart's desires
Because you my child I love and admire.
People have cursed you for way too long.
I'm going to show them that they were wrong.
Keep your eyes on me and follow your heart.
I've been directing you right from the start.
The works that you've done have not gone unseen.
My father above has wiped the slate clean.
I have so many treasures for you,
And this is what I want you to do.
Just ask of me whatever you need.
I am the one that will answer your plea.
You must know that you can ask.
And once you do, I'll complete the task.
You know you have to stand on faith.
And once you do, I am on your case.

Thressa Gillespie

YOU'RE THE APPLE OF MY EYE

All of you my children are special to me.
When I look at you a jewel is what I see.
When I think of a jewel, none are the same.
So I've given each one a special name.
You are all special in your own way.
You are such a joy I must say.
You don't have to be like anyone else.
I created you different, just be yourself.
There are so many things, I have given to you.
But if you imitate someone else, it won't be you.
Look for the good you have inside.
because as I said before...
YOU'RE THE APPLE OF MY EYE.
All of you my children are special to me.
When I look at you, a jewel is what I see.
When I think of jewels, none are the same.
So I've given each one a special name.
You are all special in your own way.
You are such a joy I must say.
You don't have to be like anyone else.
I created you different. Just be yourself.
There are so many things that I have given to you,
but if you imitate someone else, it won't be you.
Look for the good you have inside
because as I have said before, you're the apple of my eye.

MAKING THE DIFFERENCE

The things that you have done, not
one has gone unseen.
I love you my precious daughter and
I'll carry you under my wing.
You know I see your heart, and blessings
are not what you seek.
My word is in your heart, my child, and
There I know it will keep.
Oh my child, if only you knew, all
the things I will do through you.
Just continue to be this way, and hear
my child, my voice today.
You seek my face in all that you do
Because you, my daughter, know my love is true.
Anything that bothers you, come to me.
Because I came today to set you free.
Don't let the enemy burden or make you feel unsure
Because this love you've found is genuine and pure.
I don't want you to worry. Don't even have a care.
Just in case you forgot, I am always there.
Thank you my child for following me
Because I can see what you can't see.
Even when the road was bumpy and you
weren't able to see,
That's when you should rest in me.
I just want to remind you that I am always there.
No matter where you go, I am everywhere.
Be prayerful my child and don't give up hope
Because I put my strength in you so that you can always cope.

Thressa Gillespie

LOVE AT LAST

All of the time I have lost without saying that I care.
I really couldn't say it because I had no love there.
It wasn't because of you, or the things that you had done,
But I had so much pain and I had nowhere to run.
It was a long time coming before I was able to see.
I didn't have to carry the pain that God could set me free.
Forgive me of all the things that I might have done to you.
I didn't know where to hide and I didn't know what to do.
A wounded solider is what I was, but I'm not anymore.
I let God come in my life and He closed those painful doors.
I just want to love you like I never have before.
Now I'm able to see that it is so much more.
I'm taking the hate and bitterness that I hid deep inside and
I'm giving it all to God today and let Him be my guide.
All the things I wanted for you I found I couldn't afford.
The only thing I knew to do was talk to the Lord.
He told me it didn't matter what I had to spend.
A better gift for you was what I had sealed within.
Things from my heart, that no one else could give,
This is in my heart and this you're know is real.
I love you so very much and I have to make sure you know.
All of the other mess I decided to let go.
Now we can make this a brand new start,
But we all will have to do our parts.

God Said

MY CHILD

Oh my child, you are precious to me.
All the things you've done I can see.
All the prayers you prayed to me.
Not one my child, I didn't see.
You put your own problems to the side.
You were a light and became someone else's guide.
You, my child, love me just that much
You will do things as such.
My child you have a heart of gold.
I, my child, will continue to mold.
Because of the patience in you I see.
That kind of patience is a gift from me.
My child, how can I not honor your prayers?
I don't want you to be blinded of how much I care.
Stay prayed up. Read My Word
Because the people in your path will need
what you've heard.
I just need you to stay in my sight
Because I will need you to help them fight.
Just in case you are sometimes unsure,
I Love You, My child, you have nothing to fear.
Keep your head up and don't look down.
You must understand what you have found.
My Precious Child, just trust in me
Because I know all that I called you to be.

Thressa Gillespie

FAITHFUL ONE

You know my son; you are a jewel to me.
People will see me in thee.
The way you speak on my behalf is the way
they did it in the past.
You have a heart made of gold.
When you speak of me, you are so bold.
My child, when I hear you speak my word,
It's the most beautiful thing I've ever heard.
Keep on doing the things that you do.
That's why I've been blessing you.
You know you will reach some past friends.
You will speak of me and bring some of them in.
Don't let people get in your way.
Just let me show you the way.
You will be a Shepherd over my sheep,
if my word you will keep.
Just continue to keep my word in your heart; you
and my word should never apart.
You're not where I want you to be.
I will continue to set you free.
This is what I chose to do; I'm doing
this also because you asked me to.
Teach my people how not to look back.
They will be able to stay on track.
I want you, my son, go on and be blessed.
I know you will always give me your best.
I want your life to be whole and complete.
And all the things of the enemy, you will defeat.
Put my word close to your heart and that
my son will be a start.
Keep on doing my father's will, you
will make me feel it's me who lives.
When you put everything behind the word,
I know my voice, you have heard.
With people like you my kingdom will come.
My faithful son, you've already won!

God Said

GIVE IT TO ME

My child, I just want you to see that your
heart's desire can be found in me.
Of all of the hurts, you can finally be free.
Just let go and give them to me.
All of the hurt that I can see,
I came today to set you free.
All of your dreams from the past,
I desire my daughter, you have them at last.
Some of the things that you want, money
just can't buy,
and I'm not a man that I should lie.
In me you're find a love that's true.
Different from any love you ever knew.
You are my daughter and I love you so much.
I came today to fill your cup.
This kind of love does not come free.
If you want to experience it, just come to me.
I have so much love to give.
You can have it all the days that you live.
This my child is what I want to do.
This is a gift from Me, My love to you.

Thressa Gillespie

PERFECTION DESIRED

Speaking as a classmate under the sound of your voice,
Seeing your heart and giving you a choice,
To take this class and make an effort to pass
Because what you poured in could be perfected and last.
So what I want to do is write this poem for you
To remember each classmate and the hard times too.
First there is Destiny, who is eager to learn,
and doing her job is her main concern.
Then, there is a Miracle that has worked at home with
her family and loved ones on her own.
We have a woman of God who just wants to know. She
ask questions so when she leaves she will know.
My daughter, you are special, and set in your ways, but
you, my daughter, will pass with A's.
Perfection, to me is quality gold, she has
wisdom and she's not old.
Wounded is serious and she's no joke; she
likes her job and she will cope.
Determined doesn't want any less than the best, and
she won't settle for anything less.
Love is so special she's such a joy; she'll
do what is required
and she'll even do more.
Being Peaceful and quiet and eager to learn, getting
all the information is what she yearn.
Then there was Struggle, saved for last because
it was hard and I wondered if she would pass, but
because you are good at what you do, the
desire for us to pass made us work harder too.
I wrote this poem so that you won't forget. What
you've poured in is sure to stick.
Thank you God's Angel this is from your Class. We
will not forget these quality things that will last.

WORD UP

If you are looking for true love, it can be found
in the Lord above.
If you are looking for a friend, Jesus will be one
until the end.
If you are looking for a way out, that's what Jesus
is all about?
If you are wounded because of your sin,
Jesus is waiting for you to let Him come in.
If you are trying to find yourself, you don't have to
look anywhere else.
If you are blind and can't see, Jesus said that
He would lead thee.
If you are angry at the world and still in sin,
Jesus will heal you if you let Him in.
If you're tired and want to give up, Jesus said that
He would fill your cup.
If you think that the world owes you something, guess
what...you
will never have nothing.
If you think that life is not worth living, look to see
what you have been giving.
If you desire better things in life, you will have to pay a price.
Don't let your past take control of your life.
Jesus has already paid the price.
Today is the day that you can make up your mind to
show your past that your future is fine.
Let me give you some slang.
This is word just in case you haven't heard.
Take it from someone like me because I am a vessel
that Jesus set free.
I'm telling you "Word Up"! All you need is
the Master's Touch.

Thressa Gillespie

APPRECIATION POEMS

God Said

Thressa Gillespie

MY GIFT

Sometimes we forget to say how much we appreciate
you from day to day.
All the encouragement you have spoken in my life makes
my days especially nice.
All of the love that you have given to me opened my eyes
so I could see
Just how special you are to me.
The man that you see right here today, you helped to form me
in so many ways.
Positive, uplifting, wonderful words, and I sometimes felt it was
more than I deserved.
Even through sometimes, when I wanted to give up, thinking of you
was like a ministering touch.
A gift doesn't always come in a box; you're a gift to me from
the bottom to the top.
Thinking of you gives me unspeakable joy; it fulfills my heart
like never before.
I send my angels to encamp around you each day because I
love you in a special way.
Because of all you've added to my life, I can spread this joy
with my children and wife.
My heart fills this need to say, "Be Blessed. Be blessed
in a heavenly way".

EARTHLY TREASURES

I placed treasures right here on earth.
I love you my child, I loved you first.
I stayed close so you could see how sin
my child, tried to blind you from me.
I formed you my child just for me.
I have purposed for your life and plans you must see.
I know sin would never let you see who
I your father called you to be.
When I speak, "Come Forth, Come to the Light!"
No matter what life offers you, my timing is right.
Even though you think Satan is at your door.
Don't give up my child because there is more.
True treasures my child is hard to find.
But you, my child, are a treasure of mine.
Diamonds are rare; rubies are too.
Jades are special treasures just like you.
Even these jewels can't compare with you.
Because you are a treasure like man never knew,
This treasure my child, money just can't buy,
Now my child let me tell you why.
It was I who called your parents to be.
I had treasures that I needed you to see,
But I created these special treasures for me.
No formula my child can be made by man.
I came and extended my unchanging hand.
You are a treasure just for me
And that my child is how you came to be.
I created this treasure for the world to see
because you my child are a gift for me.

Thressa Gillespie

A PETITION TO HEAVEN

Sometimes words that we use everyday,
We have them in our hearts but sometimes forget to say,
Like how we appreciate each other from day to day.
When it comes to our children, it's sometimes hard to find
Someone who understands even in the hard times.
All of this joy my daughter that you have brought into my life,
I know that God has already paid the ultimate price.
I just wanted to give something very special to you,
And let you know how grateful I am to be a part of you.
I have sent prayers to heaven just for you
For blessings in your life to cover all you do.
Now as special as I think you are, the best gift
For you should come from God.
When God blesses you, He gives you more than enough,
And this child you can trust.
I sent this petition to Heavens Door
Believing God to bless you like never before.
Appreciation can be expressed in so many ways,
But I want you to remember this one everyday.

IT TAKES TWO

You are such a special part of me. When I look at you, I see me.
This Valentine's Day is a very special day.
There are so many things I've been meaning to say.
I have this love in my heart that is for only you.
No one could ever replace you no matter what they do.
When God created you, no one knew
While he was forming you, he was forming me too.
Pleased is what He was with you. He then said, "Let there be two."
I sometimes forget to say that I care.
My life would be incomplete if you were not there.
When God created you and looked at what he had done,
He said what a beautiful child. There can't just be one.
The word special can't express what I want to say.
Sweet and wonderful would be okay.
I love you in a heavenly way.
There are not many words that can express my love.
It's special like you; it comes from above.
You add such a joy to my life,
And because of you, things are twice as nice.

Thressa Gillespie

DELIVERANCE POEMS

God Said

Thressa Gillespie

PERSONAL PRAYER

John 8:36 If the son therefore shall make
You free, you shall be free indeed.

Dear Lord,
Help me to take control of this craving
I have for drugs.
Help me to turn away from drugs,
and never have the desire to go back.
Help me to love and depend
on you, and not do drugs.
Lord, help me to deal with life's problems
without feeling overwhelmed and afraid.
Help me to change my negative outlook on life
into something positive.
Lord, this is my prayer to you today,
In Jesus' name I pray,
Amen.

WHO AM I

I asked myself this question, over and over again.
I just want to know who I am, before my life ends.
I feel I'm in this web, and don't know how to get out,
I just want to know what my journey is all about.
I found this drug named Cocaine, and it became my friend,
But once I got to know it, I found it was a dead end.
Cocaine became so close to me, it was hard for me to let go.
I began to feel helpless, and had nowhere to go.
I tried to let it go, but it wouldn't leave me alone.
I told myself I didn't need this drug, but it thought I was it's home.
So now I sit back and wonder, what I'm going to do.
I began to pray, and ask God, for him to help me through.
People always tell me, you have to leave it alone,
But the desire I had for this drug, it was just so strong.
Cocaine has been a part of my life, for a very long time,
But this life that it is trying to give to me, really isn't mine.
I desire to know this man; Jesus is His Name.
But it's hard for me to know Him, because of this drug called Cocaine.
Cocaine is not my god, and it never can be,
It has nothing to offer me, even I can see.
So why is it so hard to get it out of my life?
I found it wouldn't be easy, and I just had to fight.
I have some good inside of me, but It's very hard to see, because
of this drug name cocaine who I was called to be.
God is going to deliver and totally set me free,
Because in my life's struggles, He said that to me.

Thressa Gillespie

THEY CALL ME ADDICTION

They call me addiction; I become so many people's friends.
I'm just waiting to see how I can draw you in.
Once you've let me into your life, you've then opened the door
to a deadly device.
It's as if you're digging your own grave.
You're handing me your life and you become my slave.
My name is addiction I don't care about you.
I just want to use you too.
I will make you feel that life just isn't fair.
Then I will become your worst nightmare.
Whatever I say is how it will be.
Because I have friends more popular than LSD.
We are the spirits that become your love jones.
We will get you hooked and you can't leave us alone.
You begin to think you have us under control.
But what you don't know is that I become your conscience and soul.
My name is alcohol; I come to take your youth.
I'll drain you and drain you and your appearance will be my proof.
You become dependent and don't know how to come out.
That's what addiction is all about.
You truly have the power until I am whom you choose.
And right at that very moment, in a split second, you lose!
It starts with something as small as a beer.
Understand what I'm saying, am I making my self-clear?
My name is marijuana and I just want you to see.
Once you've tried alcohol, then you will come to me.
I'll let you think you're having fun.
I'll make you forget everything you've done.
I will push you ahead as if this is not enough.
Until heroin is the one that you might want to trust.
You walk through the shadows of death and what do you see?
You haven't seen anything until you've seen me!
You've gotten your wish and it's about to come true.
I'm your worst nightmare, and this is true.
My name is Heroin I just want to get inside.
And make you wish you weren't alive!

God Said

Death; I'm telling you is right down my line.
And if you mess with addictions it will come in time!
But Cocaine my cousin is popular too.
Before this is over you'll meet him too.
Now after this is over and you choose to come our way.
Don't be surprised if this were Your Last Day!!!

Thressa Gillespie

COCAINE'S TRUTH OR CONSEQUENCES

Yeah, cocaine's my name; I'm still the same.
I'm on a mission, destroying you is my game.
I entered these countries on ships and planes.
I was sent to hell to control and deceive.
The devil is my master and your worst enemy.
Once I hit the streets I become a need.
I'm now more popular than marijuana weed.
I have people doing things they never have done.
I have them thinking they're having fun.
I've got people running here and there.
I've got them at the place that they don't care.
I have so many people lost and confused.
Cocaine is one of my destruction tools ...
So many people smoking crack.
I'm so good they keep coming back, they keep
coming back, and they keep coming back.
I'll take your loved ones and make them my fool.
I'll do with them whatever I choose.
I'll teach them new tricks, I'll teach them how to use.
Watch it people, who don't know my style.
I'll have them giving cocaine to your child.
Listen people; I'm giving you a tip.
This is the real world you better get hip.
I'll give you more than you can bear.
My name is cocaine, and I don't care!
I'll let you think you have control.
But the whole time I'll be winning your soul.
The spirit of cocaine is very strong.
I'll make you feel you're all alone.
People like you who think you can't fall.
Come on and try me I'll make you crawl.
Just try me one time I'll make sure it's good.
I'll break you down, is that understood?
I'll take school and it'll become a bore.

God Said

You know your mama; I'll make her my whore.
Yeah, I'm cocaine and I'm so bad.
I'll make you think you're losing your head.
I've got teachers and preachers who have fallen under my wing.
I rode them so well they still haven't come clean.
I know I'm bad, what can I say?
If you mess with me, it's going to be my way.
Say what you want, think what you will?
Look around and see that I am real.
I've got sons and daughters, jumping on their mothers.
I've got sisters, robbing their brothers.
I've got men and women going gay.
I make them think everything is okay.
So many babies are being born hooked.
Here are some new souls that I done took.
I'll take honest men; I'll get them hooked.
I'll take and make them society's crooks.
Yeah, I'm the man with the plans.
I want you under my command.
Now that you know, what will you do?
If you try me, this poem is for you.
Because if you don't listen to what I have to say,
you never know, this might be your last day.
Once you hear this and do it again,
if it's left up to me, it will be the end.

Thressa Gillespie

LORD HEAR MY CRY

Lord! Lord! Hear my cry.
Drugs are my suicide, don't let me die.
Lord! Lord! Are you there?
Does anybody hear me, does anyone care?
Lord if there would be one thing that I would want you to see,
it would be my heart and my desire to be free.
It boggles me how drugs can have so much control,
but yet I handed drugs my very soul.
Lord I know that you love drug addicts too.
But if we don't know, what is there for people like us to do?
Lord, any kind of drug that might have us bound.
And because of its power, our minds are not sound.
Lord if you would just answer one prayer for me.
It would be that you set your people free!
It doesn't matter where they are, or what they might be.
Lord open their eyes, that they might see.
Lord touch hearts all around the world.
Because we're all your children; and in your eyes we're pearls.
Lord, because I know you in a personal way.
There is something I want to say, Thank you Lord, Thank You.
I can say it again and again.
Because I know that you are going to bring your people out of sin.
Now being strung out on crack is where you might be.
But your heart is what God will see.
If you accept Him, He will clean you up.
Because you are His creation, and He loves you that much.
Lord, I'm asking you again to hear my cry.
Because without you Lord, we will die!

THE DOPE MAN

Yeah, I'm the devil's left hand.
I put the drugs right in your hand.
I can get you any drug that you want.
Do you understand, do you get the point?
Well, let me tell you what I really want to say.
I don't care if you OD today.
My job is not to worry about your life.
When it comes to drug addicts, I don't think twice.
All you are is a paycheck to me.
I want your money and you give it to me.
If I can just keep you on drugs.
you'll never know what it's like to be loved.
That is not all I will do, I'll take everything you own too.
When you look around everything will be gone.
Those were my plans all along.
I know just what you want me to say,
I rehearse those lines everyday.
I even act like I'm concerned, but I don't care…
when will you learn?
I'll make your children feel that they're not loved.
I'll tell them you would rather have drugs.
I'll take the time you're getting high and
I will tell them lie, after lie.
I'll sit back and wait for the money to come in, so
I can come and take it again.
Yeah, I'm the devil's left hand man; I just
don't want you to misunderstand.
I have many just like you, lost, confused
and don't know what to do.
I don't care; I'll use them too.
I have weed, crack, heroin and coke.
I have everything you want to smoke.
I have LSD or speed and BAM, I'm the
Dope Man, that's who I am.
When you see me clean as a tack, that's
your money from all of that crack.

Thressa Gillespie

My job is to take all of your pride and make you wish you weren't alive.
I will have you questioning, if your life is a mistake.
The next thing you know, it's there for me to take.
Then there is something that happens in a drug addict's life.
When they realize they have nothing to lose
they start to think twice.
They begin to wonder is this the end, or will
I die in this world of sin.
They start to wonder is there any hope or does
my life end with this
drug called dope?
Is this what I was born for?
It can't be; there has to be more!
Once they begin to look for an escape, Jesus
is the one to bring on the case.
They find a man that will set them free.
Then they think they can just leave me.
He takes people that I have controlled, and enter their
lives and makes them whole.
All of my work to them becomes old, and
then I lose another soul.
Jesus is the only one that can set you free.
That is the one person that can take you from me.
If I have to I'll give you dope free, if that's what it takes
to keep you with me.
I'll do whatever I have to do; I don't want to ever lose you.
Let me tell you, it's not because I care.
There are wounded people everywhere.
Those are the people that come to me.
They don't know Jesus can set them free.
If you really didn't know what I was here for.
Well let me tell you, I came to destroy!
If you don't believe it, come with me.
Just follow me and you will see.

God Said

WHAT DO I HAVE TO LOSE

As I look back over my past, and if that is what I would choose.
I ask myself this question, what do I have to lose?
When I look back over my past, the nights I couldn't sleep.
I remember always wondering if my soul the Lord would keep.
As I look back over my past and drugs is what I would choose.
I ask myself this question, what do I have to lose?
When I look back over my past, all the times I wished I was free, and
not knowing I had a choice, who I could really be.
When I look back over my past and all the things I've done.
I just want to say thank you God for giving your only Son.
I had asked myself this question over and over again.
Because I didn't know, I could let Jesus live within.
In my search to this question, I found that I could be used.
I then wanted to become, one of God's tools.
I asked myself this question, "Now" what do I have to lose.
Pain and a lot of hate in my life, so Christ is whom I choose.
So now that I have the answer to what I have to lose.
I now see why Satan kept me so confused.
Now that I know that I do have a choice.
I now ask the Lord to allow me to hear His voice.
Now I have made up my mind, I am so glad he chose me
for such a critical time.
There is one thing I know, one thing that I could lose.
Is being God's vessel on this earth and helping
God spread the news.

Thressa Gillespie

WANTED

These days' things have changed so much.
Most of these young children want a crutch.
They drop out of school and start to sell drugs.
They start smoking to get a "buzz".
Then, they think they really are cool.
But these are some of the devil's tools.
"I'll make them feel no one cares.
When they're down, I'll be right there."
The devil has set a trap for you.
It will go good at first, and then you're through!
Next thing you know, you'll be carrying guns.
You'll be shooting people just for fun!
They'll take people's life for a joke.
Listen to what I've said; remember what I've spoke.
The devil fixed it, he planned it that way.
He wants to destroy you, if you say "Ok.
If you open the door and let him come in.
He will being to wear you down thin."
He doesn't want you to win.
But following him could be your end.
God said that I can have what I say.
And I know my Lord will show me the way.
God said, "Don't mess with his anointed".
That the devil bit off more than he wanted.
Watch and see, my son will come in.
I got God on my side, the devil can't win!
This is a message for the youth:
I'm not going to play; I'm going to tell the truth!
I know some of you think that church is a bore.
I want you young people to keep taking score.
This is a way that it's never been said before.
Look at all the young people from before.
But God desires for you to have more.
Stand up to Satan and close that door!

Thressa Gillespie

BEREAVEMENT POEM

God Said

Thressa Gillespie

PURPOSE FULFILLED

John 14:2 There are many rooms in my father's house.
I wouldn't tell you this, unless it was true.
I am going there to prepare a place for each of you.
After I have done this, I will come back and take you with me.
Then we will be together, you know the way to where I am.

You have this special place deep down in our hearts.
And even though you have left this earth, we will never be apart.
The grave is just a holding place and your flesh returns to dust.
God has called your spirit with Him, until He comes for us.
So sad is not an option that I would choose to be.
Because I know that we will see you again, and that's a blessing to me.
All the things that you taught us and planted into our life.
Those things still work today and remembering them is so nice.
So all the wisdom that you gave us, when you
thought you were wasting your time.
Those same things you told us way back then, still come to mind.
I wish that I could tell you I love you once again.
But we will see you in heaven, when Jesus calls us in.

God Said

Thressa Gillespie

HEALING POEMS

God Said

Thressa Gillespie

FAITH IS BLIND, BUT THE SPIRIT CAN SEE

You know my child, I love you so.
You will show lost souls which way to go.
You my child will bring the captive in.
You will see them from beginning to end.
My child, I also see your heartache, and pain.
And this my child is why I came.
You know, you are a child of mine.
I see your hurt, and I'm not blind.
Watch the dangers that are about to come.
Just stop worrying you've already won.
You know how the devil work.
But I'm going to remove all of your hurt.
I see your faith and it's very strong.
There's no way that you can go wrong!
Do you think your prayers have gone unheard?
I am the Lord Jesus; I've heard every word.
To have a servant as faithful as you.
There is no way I wouldn't answer you?
You know my child, you have pleased me so.
I love you my child as I have said before.
Hold your head up, my child and don't look back.
I'm telling you now; you're on the right track.
I'm going to tell you this very day.
Just come to me; I'll show you the way.
Don't let circumstances get in your way.
I'm the same God everyday.

God Said

HALF A WOMAN

Look back over the past to see the things you've done.
During all of your life that you've lived, what really have you done?
You are getting older, what in your life has changed?
Are you doing new quality things, or are you still doing the same?
Now, if you just sit down, and look back over your life, would
you do things the same, or would you try to make a change?
You just don't have a clue of the precious jewel you are.
If your goals don't change in life, you won't get very far.
The things that you've done have no future you see.
If you want to really live, then you would come to me.
Didn't you ever wonder how your life could really be?
If you put down the drugs my child, then you can clearly see.
You're such a beautiful girl with a wonderful life ahead.
But because of the life you're living, you could very well be dead.
I came today my daughter to deliver and set you free.
I love you; my precious daughter and I want you to come to me.
Because that is the only way to see your destiny.

Thressa Gillespie

SEARCHING

When you let me come in, that will be the day
you'll find a friend.
I will stick with you to the end.
You've been running here and there.
But you can't find what you are looking for anywhere.
You can't find it in drugs or a man.
But you have it in me, your newfound friend.
I'm going to tell you that my love is true.
I won't even criticize you.
I want you to hang in there.
I'll go with you everywhere.
You have so much hurt, I know.
But you're going to have to let it go.
Come on My child and talk to me.
Because I'm going to set you free!
You don't have to carry it along.
I'll take that mess, and I'll take it home.
I want to give you peace inside.
you my child, won't have to hide.
When you open up and let me come in.
I'll know how much you love me then.
You don't have to look anymore.
I have already opened the door.
I just want you to take your time.
It's not too late, and you're just in time.
Come on My child and pick up your cross.
Follow me, so you won't get lost.
I'm going to give you a peace of mind.
As I've said before you're just in time.
I have told you what to do.
Now my child, it's up to you.
Take my advice, let it work for you.
I just want you to have a love that's true.
All the things that you can see.
If you my child just come to me.

God Said

I DARE NOT DREAM

How many of you dream? How many of you believe
that dreams can come true?
Sometime we have dreams that only God have seen.
God can birth a dream in anyone
under the sound of my voice... ANYONE

Dream is something I dared not do, because of the life I lived.
What kind of life could I have had, when I had nothing to give?
I didn't even have the desire to live, why would my dreams come true.
Dreams were strangers in my life, dreams I never knew.
I found this void deep inside, love was what I yearned.
I didn't know where to find it; I didn't know where to turn.
I carried the desire in my heart, I carried it oh so deep.
I didn't know that God loved me, and my soul that He would keep.
When I heard about this God I didn't know what to do.
My hearts desire was to know this man, I heard His love was true.
He then introduced His self to me, and began to set me free.
All the dreams I didn't have, He began to give to me.
First He began to heal the pain that I had carried oh so long.
He wiped the tears from my eyes, and let the pain be gone.
He then began to give me dreams and they all came so fast.
All the dreams that He gave to me, began to come to past.
But now I'm able to dream, and know that they can come true.
God can place a dream in you, and they will come true too.
So take the dare out of your dream, and let that be a start.
Just step out of the way, remove yourself and let God do His part.
Since God has become apart of my life and allowed me to dream.
What a wonderful life I have, a life that's filled with dreams.
The Lord began to minister to me; He said it was time for change.
God has no respect of person, and He loves you just the same.
He's given a dream to all of us, no matter how big or small.
Don't let not one of your dreams be lost, don't let not one dream fall.
Dreams are not impossible, there things you've not yet done.
But now that you know that dreams can come true completing them is the fun.

Thressa Gillespie

Don't let people cloud your dreams, or make you give up hope.
Sometimes their life is without a dream, and they don't know how to cope.
So now that you know, that dreams can come true, and having them is okay.
We can be a light to other, and help them find their way.

God Said

AT LAST

My child it took you a while, but I knew you were coming because you are my child.
You my child are on the right track, just remember, and don't look back.
The devil will try to keep you in the past.
He doesn't want you to give up his mask.
You have been in back too long.
That's not my plan for you, and it's all wrong.
Don't worry about what people say.
Because before it's over you will show them the way.
The devil will use people to make you feel bad.
But don't keep those thoughts in your head.
Just remember I'm always there.
You can give me all of your cares.
I have heard your prayers from so far back.
I just want you to know I haven't forgotten.
I'm letting you know it has all added up.
Now I'm going to fill your cup!
You my child have been through so much.
I want to give you My Loving Touch.
All of those people that think they know you so well.
Just don't know you've been going through hell.
I know your hurt and I know it goes deep.
This pain my daughter you no longer have to keep.
I know the truth; I want to set you free.
Because there are no secrets you can keep from me.
I'm about to set you free because you my daughter came to me.
I'm going to show you what I can do.
I'm going to do it just for you.
I've been waiting for you so long.
Don't let the devil steer you wrong.
Just know you're not missing anything.
You my daughter are going to be my beautiful Black Queen.

Thressa Gillespie

LETTING GO

I didn't know the meaning of a bundle of love.
Until God sent my daughter from up above.
That was the happiest day in the world.
Because God had sent me two beautiful little girls.
You know letting go was hard for me.
But now God said He's setting me free.
All this hurt, I hid it so well.
There was no way people knew the pain I felt.
There was so much pain that they couldn't see.
So they didn't know what it was doing inside of me.
I didn't think people would understand.
Just what I was really saying.
To my daughters I want you to rest.
Because of my lifestyle it was for the best.
You are with God in heaven you see.
That's where you are going to see me.
Jesus will show me the way
because in His word that is what he say.
All of the unforgiveness that I have inside.
I'm giving it to God and let him be my guide.
God uproots the old, and He plants the new.
He wants to do the same for you.
No other man can do this you see.
Because he is the only one who died for you and me.
He took all of our hurt to the cross.
So that our souls wouldn't have to be lost.
What a mighty God we serve.
I think his love is much deserved.
That's why God set us free.
So we could love Him willingly.

God Said

FOLLOW ME

I just want to make sure you know, everything
in your past, I have forgiven at last.
You don't have to hold it anymore.
I came today to close that door.
Today my son I want to set you free.
Pick up your cross and follow me.
All of your prayers I have heard.
My son I've heard every word.
All of your gifts that you could use.
But if you pass you could lose.
All of those shackles, I can set you free.
If you my son would come to me.
I've planned your life from the beginning to the end.
I love you my son until the end.
All of the dreams you will see.
If you pick up your cross and follow me.
This can be the beginning of a brand new life.
One that is loving, peaceful and nice.
Son if you just want to be free.
Pick up your cross and follow me.

Thressa Gillespie

ANOTHER CHANCE

Satan came for you once before.
I'm the one that closed the door.
You are my child and I love you so.
It's not time for you to go.
You have a new found life.
You have become your husband's wife.
You have to fight everyday to get free.
That shows me how much you love me.
Don't give up on your married life.
He is your husband and you are his wife.
When you got married and said "I DO".
You were saying I'd fight for you too.
He's going to be a real man.
I know how you feel...I do understand.
My son I've heard you say that you are the man.
But you my son must take a stand.
Be the man that you really are.
Stop the devil before he goes too far.
My son I have so many blessings for you.
And there is work for you to do.
You can't run and you can't hide.
It's all right to drop your pride.
Married life is not the same.
It is time to stop playing games.

God Said

Be a husband to your wife.
You will have the best life.
You are young and so alive.
Follow me and I will be your guide.
I will not tell you anything wrong.
I just want your life to be prosperous and long.
I want you to stand and fight.
Your wife does it day and night.
You shouldn't let her do it alone.
As husband and wife it's all wrong.
You and your wife should stick together.
Because that's the way I planned it in heaven.
You can do this, I know you can.
Come on my son and be a man.

Thressa Gillespie

QUALITY GOLD

There is nothing wrong with being old.
You bless people, you're quality gold.
If people really looked deep inside,
they will find much wisdom and a positive guide.
Age is nothing you should regret,
I came today to tell you that you're God's best.
When I look at older people, I see beauty,
wisdom, learning, strength and more,
I see things that are to me a tremendous joy!
Even if you feel you have no worth,
Jesus loves you He planned your birth.
Jesus came to let you know,
that you're special to Him and He loves you so.
He just came to heal you today; He'll be your guide,
he'll show you the way.
He came to set you free,
He says, "my daughter, just come to me."

God Said

I FORGIVE

I finally realized that you had no control.
Of the time and day you lost your soul.
My only prayer for you today.
Is that God received your soul that day.
The day you died my life came to an end.
But then I realized a new life began.
So many changes I had to make.
I had to do it for my children's sake.
You know I learned a lot from you.
You taught me how to fight, and hide hurt too.
I'm not saying it was wrong.
I'm just saying I carried the hurt so long.
I didn't know what a good mother should be.
I just did what was done to me.
I met someone that really loves me.
His name is Jesus; He's setting me free.
All the hurt and pain I had, was because most
of my life I was very sad.
I found out something I never knew before.
God is not just a picture, He's so much more!
Do you know what the best part was?
God sent His son with so much love?
I never knew what real love was.
I mean the love from God above.
I never knew I felt this way.
I just learned about this today.
Everything that God has allowed me to see.
He's telling me that He's setting me free.
I know I will make it through this fight.
Pray that I stay in the Lord's sight.
The devil has fought me from the beginning to the end.
Because even He knows, I'm going to win!
I wrote this poem when I was lost.
But I knew Jesus paid the cost.
Lord, I know that you really care.
I know in my past you were always there.
I'll close this poem today in faith.
Because I know God is on my case.

Thressa Gillespie

BROKEN

Bro-ken is not just a word I heard, but to me it's
so much more, Bro-ken was my life before I met
Christ, and he became my Lord.
Just as you would drop a glass and each piece
would going its way, that was my life before I met
Christ going in so many different ways. Then God
Looked down at my bro-ken soul and He began to
mold. That's my child and I love her so and this she
has to know. He began to fit each piece so
carefully in place, he then began to mend this
vessel and I became his case.
He took this bro-ken vessel and did what he
does best. He began to heal the bro-ken-ness
and remove all the mess. He spoke to this
bro-ken vessel and commanded it to be whole, and
right at that very moment the vessel began to
mold. Just a few touches and the vessel was
completely whole. That's the kind of God
we serve, he wants us all complete and whole
Once he finishes molding us then our souls
he'll keep. So if you ever feel broken
and don't know what to do, just give
your life to Christ today, and he will
mold you too.

COME IN

I remember what it was like the day you entered my life.
I didn't know I needed you, but I knew things just weren't right.
I knew that something was missing, but I didn't know what it was.
I knew one thing that I hadn't gotten was a lot of needed love.
Lord you knew what I needed and you knew just what to do.
When I was ready to end my life, that's when I met you.
I thank you God so very much for the day He gave us you.
Suicide was the only thing I knew I could do.
From the day that I received you my life has really changed.
And because of you, I know, it will never be the same.
You have healed so much hurt in me, and I now know why you came.
I take my life more seriously, because it's you that lives in me.
I surrender myself, all of me, so that you can set me free.
I found out that you were real, and on this very earth you live.
Not only do you have a love that heals, but this love I've found is also real.
It feels your hurt and emptiness, and makes your dreams come true.
God will direct your every step and rebuke the devour for you.
Jesus you know this poem I write can be for no one but you.
There is not one person on this earth that can do the things you do.
I just want to thank you, over and over again.
For that very special moment, that I allowed you to come in.

Thressa Gillespie

REAL LOVE

You my son have so much pride; I just want to be your guide.
I just want you to begin to pray, and you must do this everyday.
You always say that you need new clothes, just seek me; I'll give you those.
If you just didn't move so fast, all of your desires would come to past.
Can't you see how the devil works; he doesn't want you to come to church.
There is so much good in you and there is so much that you can do.
Don't you know that your life is not yours, and I can open so many doors.
All of the things that you asked me for; I can give you that and more.
All that you want to be, I am the one that has the key.
You will run around each day, and you will search until you come my way.
I know you love your brother so much, but you can no longer be his crutch.
I want him to come to me; it is time to set him free.
I love you and your brother so much, and I want to give you
my loving touch.
You've been hurt and you have to be healed.
But you must come to me of your own free will.
I want to show you what love is; I have so much my son to give.
I want to reach way down inside and take the pain you're trying to hide.
You don't have to be in fear, I, the Lord God, caught every tear.
You have trouble showing love, it's a gift from up above.
You want love but you can't see, it just won't work until I set you free.
I'll be with you until the end; I'm not like your so-called friends.
Open your eyes and be aware, the people you call your friends
really don't care.
Bow your head and raise your voice, let the devil know
that I am your choice.
The devil will blind you so you can't see, and when you look
around you might not be free.

God Said

WHERE IS THE LOVE

The love that I was searching for, I never found in drugs.
It wasn't in the men that I met, or in the making love.
The kind of love that I wanted was hard for me to find.
The kind of love I searched for, was a very special kind.
It couldn't just come from anywhere or fall right into my life.
The kind of love I needed, had to be precise.
Everywhere that I looked, love was never there.
I found myself running, looking everywhere!
GOD knew that I was looking, in places love didn't live.
And in the places that I was looking, they had no love to give.
Everybody's searching for one thing or other.
But you just don't give up, look a little further.
GOD knew what I wanted, and I needed it all the time.
So HE just gave HIS love to me, and HE said that it was mine.
Though HE began to direct the path in which I should go.
I was still out searching, I didn't even know.
The love that I was searching for, that Love I craved so deep.
GOD had already decided that HE would direct my feet.
I didn't know that God had this special love to give.
HE said that I could keep it, because it's HE in me that lives.
All of the love that He gave me, oh it felt so good.
But there was something missing if only I understood.
Then, the Lord, spoke to me and told me what was wrong.
I didn't know how to receive this love, I wanted oh so long.
Love was what I wanted, but to me it was something new.
And when He gave His love to me I didn't know what to do.
I felt that HE had given me something, that I couldn't give back.
But I knew that love was a two-way thing so I tried to give His love back.
One way that I can show my love is to try to stay on track.
So if you want a love, that has no strings attached.
Come to know this God that I know.
HE gives a love like that!

Thressa Gillespie

HOLD ON

I don't want you to give up; I want you to know
I love you so much.
The devil doesn't want to let you go, he wants you
to stand at the door.
But that's not enough my friend, I want you
to come all the way in.
I want to set you totally free; I want you my son
to work for me.
I'm going to tell you this today, I my son
am the only way.
Anything you ask for… I can open the door.
Aren't you tired of that life you had, don't
you want to let it stay dead?
You deserve so much more, I just want to give you joy.
All the dreams that you had can come true, surrender
to me and become brand new.
Come on my son make this the day, come on and
let me show you the way.

HIDDEN LOVE

I can never repay you, for all the tears that you have cried.
For all the tears that you sent up just for me to survive.
I just want to tell you that I was hurting too.
I didn't know how to love you so I just hurt you too.
Expressing my feelings is hard for me.
I'm sure that you can see, that's not me but a wounded
soldier is not whom I've been called to be.
I just want you to know, you can never be repaid.
Without you in my life, I would be a helpless case.
I'm glad that the Lord has delivered you, and set you free.
You went out to check the waters to make sure it was all right for me.
You always went out ahead of me, to make sure that the way was clear.
Making sure everything was all right so I would have nothing to fear.
Thank you for all the time that you took to invest in me.
I'm going to do the same for you, you just wait and see.

Thressa Gillespie

BE HEALED

You know my son; you've come a long way.
I remember the things that you used to say.
You didn't think you were any good.
You couldn't find anyone that understood.
You began to let go and give it to me.
Now I can begin to set you free.
You finally began to let down your guard.
Now, I can begin to heal your heart.
All the pain that you didn't want anyone to see.
Today I'm going to set you free.
You are my son and I love you so.
This is something that I want you to know.
Blessed are the ones that keep My Word.
And you my son I have heard.
All of the prayers that you prayed.
I want you to know I heard you each day.
I'm about to change your life.
This will bless you and your wife.
You know your wife is such a joy.
She is more joyful than ever before.
You know, my child I love you too.
Watch and see the things I do.
All of the blessing that I have in store for you.
They are going to overwhelm you!
You know my child I will deliver and set you free.
I'm going to heal all the hurt that I see.
No more of this hurt will you have to feel.
That aching heart I'm going to heal!
You have carried that pain for so long.
My blessing to you is that it all be gone.
All of the prayers you've prayed alone.
I heard them my son I want it to be known.
I my son will honor every one; this word is for you my son.
Don't come back to get them again.
I will carry them until the end.
You know your burdens, my child are light.

God Said

you my child will do what is right.
When you met me you met a friend.
and I will be there until the end.
You just call me and I'll be right there.
Because I'm your Father, and yes I care.
For your wife, I'll give her a brand new life.
Because she my son is paying the price.
You are blessed my children and I love you so.
I will always show you which way to go.

Thressa Gillespie

BLINDED

My daughter, I just want you to see, I
have already healed thee.
If you're not sure of what I say, drop to
your knees my child, and pray.
Understand my Words and what I say.
Confess my Word from day to day.
The anointing my child is what breaks the yoke.
My word and your faith, and it is broke!
Do you know what you mean to me?
My desire my child is that you be set free.
If you my child would do these things.
Once again my miracles will be seen.
You know this is only a test.
And you my daughter just have to ask.
If healing is what you need from me.
Speak those things and you will see.
My daughter there is no need to waiver.
Because you my child have my favor.

God Said

BROKEN HEARTED

Proverbs 3:5-6 trust in the Lord with all your heart and Lean not on your own understanding; in all your ways acknowledge him, and he will make your paths straight.

It's time for me to heal the pain you have received.
I want you to step out because I'm what you need.
The friends I will send you are like no one from the past.
But I will send you new friends, the kind my child that last.
There is nothing wrong with you, but you need friends that are true.
I'm going to give you peace inside; you no longer have to hide.
There is healing you need too, I my child will bring you through.
You're no different from anyone else; you have to start to love yourself.
Come on my child surrender it to me, today I'm going to set you free!
You and your wife must both be free.
You'll both have real friends- just wait and see.
I can see all of your pain, and this is the reason that I came.
Come on my children; let's get out of the past.
You're going to have true friends at last.

Thressa Gillespie

YOU'RE SPECIAL

Sometimes you forget, how much I really care.
And if you ever need me I'll always be right there.
There will always be a place deep in my heart for you.
And this is the best love that I ever knew.
I knew that you were special and a gift from up above,
I thank God for this wonderful gift; he gave us this bundle of love.
That was one of my dreams that you helped bring to pass.
That has blessed by life with a joy that will last.
If I had another chance to choose all over again.
There wouldn't be a choice for me I would choose you again.
No matter what we go through or even how it looks.
There will always be a special place in my heart.
If you just take the time to look.

SALVATION

Salvation for me is being set free.
That is what salvation has done for me.
It gave me a chance to make a change.
I no longer have to be ashamed.
When light began to come inside.
I knew I could no longer hide.
Once I stopped and began to see.
I saw salvation glowing in me.
I see things like never before.
Salvation has opened a brand new door!
It's like a blind man getting his sight.
He comes out of the dark and into the light.
Salvation is learning who you are.
And with God, you don't have to look very far.
God has called us from the womb.
He just wants us to prosper and bloom.
Salvation doesn't let you settle for less.
When you come out of bondage you want only the best!
Salvation is what the Lord gave me.
This is who He called me to be.
Now, I can tell the devil to flee.
The Lord has given me victory!
He will do the same for you.
And this is a gift I know to be true.
It doesn't have to be any other way.
The Lord is giving you this word today.
Salvation has brought me a mighty long way.
You will think about this again one day.
The word salvation can go forever.
Because my Savior is very clever.
Don't let anything get you down.
You have salvation; you're no longer bound!
You tell that devil to just shut up.
Because the Lord is the one who fills your cup.
I don't want you to look down again.
No matter how it looks you're going to win!

Thressa Gillespie

Now that you know what you've got.
You don't have any reason to go back.
Now that you know that you have come out.
There's no room for you to doubt.
Now that salvation has set you free.
Take all your problems and give them to me.
Don't come back and take them again.
Give them to me and fight till the end.
I will be there when you finally win.
Let your salvation finally begin.

God Said

BRO-KEN LO-VE

All of the pain you don't want anyone to see.
I came today to set you free.
All of the hurt you're trying to hide.
I came today that I might be your guide.
You know my child I love you so much.
I want you to have My Loving Touch.
All of the pain you've carried so long.
Come to Me, I have a song.
Jesus loves you I hope you know.
But if you didn't I'm telling you so.
I just want you to come to me.
Your hearts desire is to be set free.
Loneliness is not what I planned for you.
Spend time with me; I'll bring you through.
All of the things I have for you.
Oh my daughter if you only knew!
Man can't give you the things I have.
A job, can't give it to you my child.
Come to see what I have for you.
And this love I have my child, is true.
I called you from your mother's womb.
I want you to prosper and to bloom.
You are a gift to me my child.
Your countenance alone, make me smile.
I want you to know who I created you to be.
Because in me you can be set free!
All of the things you've asked me for.
I want to give you that and more.
Don't you settle for anything less.
Because I, My child want to give you my best.

Thressa Gillespie

ALONE

When I was a child, I couldn't wait to get grown.
But when I thought grown, I didn't think alone.
I thought then, all the pain would be gone.
There's this void, it's been there so long.
Only God can fix the part that is wrong.
I can't quite touch it, but it's something not there.
I've been searching for it everywhere.
Well I finally met Christ and I can say today
He has changed my life.
The life before could not compare.
God gave me hope that was never there.
Now that I've met him, I don't want to let go.
But my past won't leave me; it camps out at my door.
I never knew what freedom entailed.
But it's a job for me to stay out of hell.
Now that I have already come in.
I know that I have to fight to the end.
I just want to stay clean and free.
The Lord said He gave that to me.
I know my God He doesn't lie.
But when problems come I feel the need to get high.
I know God isn't the author of drugs and mess.
But it's been hard for me trying to pass this test.
How can I get rid of all these things?
There is nothing wrong with just living clean.
Lord you know what I need and you know why.
All that I'm going through I just want to cry.
I feel that I'm at a dead end road.
If only things would just begin to unfold.
I know I can't do it alone.
But why when I feel like this everything goes wrong.
I don't want to live in my past any more.
I just want to close that painful door.
Lord there's nothing more that I can do.
I raise my hands and surrender today.
The only thing I know to do, is step out of your way

God Said

so you can bring me through.
All I have to do is have peace and rest.
And allow you to help me pass this test.
When I began to feel I had nowhere to turn.
Then it was my past that I would yearn.
I'm just telling you this happened to me.
I had to work in order to stay free.
I really thought I had got through that.
But before I knew it I had went back.
Then I felt so bad inside, all I wanted to do was hide.
I exposed the devil to some of my friends.
I knew it had to come to an end.
It's not over, but it's going to be.
Because the Lord told me He was setting me free.
Now I have made it through my fifth year.
I now know I heard God and His voice was clear.

Thressa Gillespie

VALENTINE POEMS

God Said

Thressa Gillespie

MY LOVE

There's something I have been meaning to say.
I love you more everyday.
This love that I have doesn't come in a box.
There's not enough room, you're just too hot!
The love that you have is not in the store.
it wouldn't last long; they would request more..................
Your love is unique and so very nice,
Your love could not be labeled with a price.
This kind of gift comes from God.
He knows the desires of our hearts.
You know, I know what you mean.
This is the same thing I have seen.
This same kind of love I see in you.
I didn't know you saw this in me too.
God had to put us together,
Because this kind of love comes straight from heaven.

God Said

CAN'T NOBODY LOVE YOU LIKE ME

John 3:16
For God so loved the world, that he gave his only
Begotten son, that whosoever believeth in him
Should not parish, but have everlasting life.

Can't nobody love you like Me, I died to set you free, Be Mine.
I called you my child, I called you by name, and
because of this you'll never be the same.
Can't nobody love you like Me, Be Mine.
I picked you up and turned you around, when you
came to me you were found.
Can't nobody love you like Me, Be Mine.
When you thought things were at a dead end, I didn't
leave you I was there then.
Can't nobody love you like Me, Be Mine.
I opened your eyes so that you could see, I love
you my child, that was me.
Can't nobody love you like Me, Be Mine.
I came to earth so that you can be free, when people
see you, they would see me.
Can't nobody love you like Me, Be Mine.
I'll keep you safe from all harm; follow me
until my kingdom come.
Can't nobody love you like Me. Be Mine.
I'll take your past, so that you can be free, that's
the way I said it would be.
Can't nobody love you like Me, Be Mine.
I can make all your dreams come true, that's
what I want to do for you.
Can't nobody love you like Me, Be Mine.
I love you my child, I just want to make sure that you see.
Can't nobody love you like Me, Be Mine.

Thressa Gillespie

BE MY VALENTINE

Valentine's to me was just another day, until a special love came my way.
That was the day that I came alive, so many new feelings I found inside.
There was something missing in my life, until the day that you became my wife.
You know dreams really do come true, I know because God has sent me you.
Now...
That was to me an unspeakable joy: I experience feelings like never before.
To me, my daughter you are a queen: and my son you are a child of a King.
This Valentines Day is like none of the rest, because
today my children it will be your best.

God Said

Thressa Gillespie

PASTOR POEMS

God Said

Thressa Gillespie

SENT BY GOD

This gift that I have to give you money just can't buy.
Let me write this poem for you, and let me tell you why.
This poem that I have written can be for no one but you.
There's not another person that has done the things you do.
I spent a long time looking, for people just like you.
Someone that would love me for once in
my life and show me what to do.
Someone that saw something, no one else could see.
Someone that gave me hope and a chance to let God set me free.
You stayed by me, prayed for me, and never gave up hope.
Because of the trust that you put in me; I
have the strength to cope.
When God put you under His wings, that was a
blessing only He could have seen.
I just want you to know how much you mean to me.
You helped me to see who God called me to be.
I never felt love before, I always felt so blue.
I'm finally beginning to feel love, I learned from the two of you.
I never thought strangers could change my life so much.
But I thank God for people like you, for loving me so much.
You brought out something in my life that I never knew was there.
You let me know, that it was all right, for people like me to care.
All of the hurt that I had inside, that I thought I could hide.
I would still be holding it, if I didn't have you as my guide.
I just want to say thank you for everything you've done.
Because of your love and trust in me, I feel I've already won.

God Said

PURE GOLD

I called you pastor, I called you by name.
When you preach My Word, I preached it the same.
All the love you have for me, only your true sheep can see.
I chose you to shepherd my sheep.
And my word, I know you will keep.
You do not let one man cause you to
waiver and because of that you have my favor.
I am so pleased when you bring people together,
because I see souls coming up to heaven.
People will try to lead you astray, but you know me
you know the way.
There will be drug addicts, rapists and drug dealers and more.
You'll see all kinds of people, coming through your doors.
You will be preaching to a new found gold.
Once you begin feeding them, my gifts will unfold.
All the people I'll send my son, will work to help
My kingdom come.
Watch the sheep that you will lead, these special
sheep, anyone can't feed.
You will make them strong and stern and for me, they
will yearn.
No weapon formed against you shall prosper.
I'm telling you because I'll make it impossible.
My son, keep your eyes on me.
There are so many things for you to see.
Just be a vessel and set my people free.

Thressa Gillespie

RESTORATION POEMS

God Said

Thressa Gillespie

WAIT I SAY ON THE LORD

God should be the center of the life of a woman and man.
Because when God created one that was His plan.
I came to tell you how God's plan could go wrong,
and that is if you try to find your mate on your own.
Say there's a woman that is ready to become a wife
and she puts God second place in her life.
Because of her choice; she'll have to pay the price.
Because she has given the devil room in her life.
The devil has a mate planned just for you.
And he will have a counterfeit, when you say I do.
He will have you questioning if this man is for you.
And have you believing that this love is true.
But the man God has for you is still following Christ.
And He knows that God has promised Him a wife.
Knowing that his wedding will come to pass
and by keeping God in the center it will last.
Because she decided not to hear God's voice,
she will miss him because she's off course.
Or if it were the other way around
his given wife would not be found.
The Bible says, He who finds a wife finds a good thing.
But if you're off course, you can't be seen.
Because this man trusted God with his life.
God will send him another wife.
Never knowing about losing God's first choice.
He will marry the second one because he hears God's voice.
But if they both put God first.
This marriage that God planned will then be birthed.

God Said

I'LL SEND HIM

There are reasons to why your mate hasn't come;
just for your peace I'm preparing my son.
This is for the two of you.
This wedding will not come until I'm through.
Let your worries come to an end.
Because your mate I will send.
And your newfound life will then begin.
My daughter, I just want to make sure you understand.
For you to have a mate was part of my plan.
When I created Adam, I knew he needed Eve.
And I called her forth and I was pleased.
Before you even knew who I was.
I had ordained you this special love.
Before you even came to earth.
I spoke your future to come to birth.
I am God and I said, "Let There Be".
My word can't come back void to me.
I just spoke the words "Let There Be"
And the Words then became a living seed.
I the Lord God knows just what you need.
And that's what your mate is going to be.
This man I am sending is for you.
And his love my daughter will be true.
But first my daughter I must prepare you.
All the things that happened in your past.
You have to be healed so your marriage will last.
I don't want you to settle for less.
But for you my child, I will give my best.
Don't be impatient and go astray.
Because your mate is on the way!
Listen my daughter to what I say,
to this word that I'm sending you on this day.
Just stay in My Word My child and pray.
And let my word minister to your spirit today.
You can have a love that's true.
Because that will be my gift to you.

Thressa Gillespie

Your mate my daughter must be primed.
Before my daughter this jewel he will find.
My daughter, I know your heart's desire.
I am God your Father, the Messiah.
My daughter I beseech you, don't be deceived.
To me my daughter you shall cleave.

God Said

GOD CAN'T LIE

Did I not tell you, my daughter, and my son?
That your mate I've spoken of is going to come!
Did I not tell you, I said (" Let There Be").
And my word can't come back void to me!
I told you my daughter that my son is on the way.
What else my child, do I have to say?
A man is not what will make your love true.
But that's what I will bring in the two of you.
All of life's hurts that you've tried to hide.
The reality is; it's hidden inside.
That is why I want you free.
I can heal you, if you wait on me.
I'm not a man, that I should lie.
And you my child keep asking me why!
Where is the faith that you said you had in me?
And if I said it, then (Let It Be)!
Did I not tell you, there are things that I must do.
Before I send your mate to you.
Let's say that you feel that you can't wait.
For the time I need to heal your mate;
And you both come together, and you're both undone.
Then I have a wounded daughter, and a wounded son.
There's no way that you can be one!
But here you are, thinking your mate will bring it together.
But what you need is a touch from heaven.
When you stop and realize that he's only a man.
And My Healing process was a much-needed plan.
Then you want to put it back in my hands!
If you my son, and daughter, want a love that's true,
wait until I send, your mate to you!

Thressa Gillespie

TRUST ME

You ask me for a mate, and you want him to be good.
But when I said Wait On Me, it's not understood.
You want this man to be with you for the rest of your life.
But you act like you can't wait to become a wife.
My daughter I said I want to give you my best
but if you want him now, you'll have to settle for less.
I said that I would give you a love that's true.
And that my daughter is what I'm going to do.
You want real love, and that takes time.
I'm patient with these creations of mine.
Perfection can only be found in me.
And that's how I desire your future to be.
Love is something that's nurtured and true.
That's what I am preparing everyday for you.
What I have for you is all in my plans.
And everything my daughter, you don't have to understand.
I love you my daughter, what else must I say?
You will begin to understand on your wedding day.
Your future was planned before you even came to earth.
I spoke your future before your birth.
I am God and I created the heavens and the earth.
And you act like I didn't call you to be birthed.
I called your mate, yes, I called him too.
I have a man that will understand and love you.
There are married people out here today
that is regretting their wedding day.
There are also women with mates, that will not
listen to what they have to say.
They have thoughts of killing him one day.
Is this what you want your future to be?
You deserve so much more, just wait on me.
My daughter, all kinds of things are happening in this world.
But I know your mate that's who I am preparing.
My daughter, if you just trust in me.
Then your future I've spoken of is going to be.

God Said

Tell your flesh to take a back seat.
Because I'm in control of your wedding being complete.
So if you want the things that I say, let
Me perfect your wedding day.

Thressa Gillespie

BEHOLD MY SON, BE WHOLE

Proverbs 18:22
He who finds a wife finds a good thing
And obtains favor from the Lord

I call wholeness unto you.
A complete vessel, a man renewed.
Healing my son is what you need
because of life's empty seeds.
I speak wholeness into your life
before my son you find your wife.
I will uproot the old and plant the new.
There is some fertilizing I must do.
Spiritual surgery on your inner parts.
Place inside a godly heart.
Reprogram your teaching from the world
because my teaching is not like theirs.
Plant My Word deep in your soul.
Once it's rooted, I'll call my creation up whole!
Oh my son, what a joy this will be, when your
new spirit I can see!
On the day that I had finished the earth
I then thought, there must; be a birth.
Someone in flesh in the image of Me, and
that my son is how you came to be.
I began to form you from the dust.
Blew in your nostrils and there you were.
I looked and saw what I had done.
There in My Image was you my son.
I looked and said that was good, but the next
miracle I would do, you never understood.
Man was on the earth, not knowing he needed a mate.
But what a gift he would have when he awaked.
So, when I spoke let there be two.
I carved the woman out of you
I did surgery and took out a rib, and
because of this the woman lives.

God Said

My son I'm calling you back to me.
Because now it's time to set you free.
I myself called marriage to be.
Because marriage my son is a gift from me!